_____

From

_____

Date

_____

Fifty
Shades
of Grace

*Devotions Celebrating
God's Unlimited Gift*

The quoted ideas expressed in this book (but not Scripture verses) are not, in all cases, exact quotations, as some have been edited for clarity and brevity. In all cases, the author has attempted to maintain the speaker's original intent. In some cases, quoted material for this book was obtained from secondary sources, primarily print media. While every effort was made to ensure the accuracy of these sources, the accuracy cannot be guaranteed. For additions, deletions, corrections, or clarifications in future editions of this text, please write Freeman-Smith.

Scripture quotations are taken from:

The Holy Bible, King James Version (KJV)

The Holy Bible, New International Version (NIV) Copyright © 1973, 1978, 1984, by International Bible Society. Used by permission of Zondervan Publishing House. All rights reserved.

The Holy Bible, New King James Version (NKJV) Copyright © 1982 by Thomas Nelson, Inc. Used by permission.

Holy Bible, New Living Translation, (NLT) copyright © 1996. Used by permission of Tyndale House Publishers, Inc., Wheaton, Illinois 60189. All rights reserved.

The Message (MSG)- This edition issued by contractual arrangement with NavPress, a division of The Navigators, U.S.A. Originally published by NavPress in English as THE MESSAGE: The Bible in Contemporary Language copyright 2002-2003 by Eugene Peterson. All rights reserved.

New Century Version®. (NCV) Copyright © 1987, 1988, 1991 by Word Publishing, a division of Thomas Nelson, Inc. All rights reserved. Used by permission.

The Holy Bible, The Living Bible (TLB), Copyright © 1971 owned by assignment by Illinois Regional Bank N.A. (as trustee). Used by permission of Tyndale House Publishers, Inc., Wheaton, Illinois 60189. All rights reserved.

International Children's Bible®, New Century Version®. (ICB) Copyright © 1986, 1988, 1999 by Tommy Nelson™, a division of Thomas Nelson, Inc. All rights reserved. Used by permission.

The New American Standard Bible®, (NASB) Copyright © 1960, 1962, 1963, 1968, 1971, 1972, 1973, 1975, 1977, 1995 by The Lockman Foundation. Used by permission.

The Holman Christian Standard Bible™ (HCSB) Copyright © 1999, 2000, 2001 by Holman Bible Publishers. Used by permission.

Cover Design by Kim Russell / Wahoo Designs
Page Layout by Bart Dawson

ISBN 978-1-60587-427-2

Printed in the United States of America

1 2 3 4 5—CGH—16 15 14 13 12

Fifty Shades of Grace

Devotions Celebrating God's Unlimited Gift

For by grace you are saved through faith, and this is not from yourselves; it is God's gift— not from works, so that no one can boast.

—

Ephesians 2:8-9 Holman CSB

Introduction

God does not change, but we human beings are in a constant state of flux. So, we experience differing shades of grace depending upon our own unique personalities and our own particular circumstances. Yet, even though we may experience God's gifts in different ways, nothing can alter the fact that God is steadfast today, tomorrow, and forever.

You inhabit a world that glorifies (and values) things that are temporary (wealth, physical appearance, fame, and youth, for starters), but your heavenly Father knows better. He glorifies women who build their lives on the things that are eternal: God's love, God's grace, God's promises, God's Son, and the priceless gift of eternal life through Him.

How desperately our world needs Christian women who are willing to honor God with their praise, their prayers, and their service. Hopefully, you are determined to be such a woman—a woman who walks in wisdom as she offers counsel and direction to her family, to her friends, and to her coworkers.

In your hands, you hold a book that contains 50 devotional readings about God's love and God's grace.

During the next 50 days, please try this experiment: read a chapter each day. If you're already committed to a daily worship time, this book will enrich that experience. If you are not, the simple act of giving God a few minutes each morning will change the direction and the quality of your life.

As you consider your own circumstances, remember this: whatever the size of your challenge, whatever the scope of your problem, God is bigger. Much bigger. He will instruct you, protect you, energize you, and heal you if you let Him. So let Him. Pray fervently, listen carefully, work diligently, and treat every single day as an opportunity for praise and worship because that's precisely what every day can be . . . and should be.

Shades of Grace

For all have sinned, and fall short of the glory of God, being justified freely by His grace through the redemption that is in Christ Jesus....

Romans 3:23-24 NKJV

We human beings are similar in many ways, but each of us is unique. Each of us possesses a unique array of talents and opportunities gifted from the Father above. Because of our uniqueness, we all experience God's grace in somewhat different ways—we experience different shades of grace depending upon our own circumstances, our own temperaments, and our own personal histories. For example, the fidgety sixteen-year-old runaway who accepts Christ may experience a different collection of emotions than the mature 80-year-old grandmother who has spent the last seven decades in the service of her Heavenly Father. But even though we mortals experience God's grace in different ways, nothing can alter the fact that God is unchanging, and so, for that matter, are His promises.

Romans 3:23 reminds us that all of us fall short of the glory of God. Yet despite our imperfections and despite our shortcomings, God sent His Son so that we might be redeemed from our sins. In doing so, our Heavenly Father demonstrated His infinite mercy and His infinite love.

Christ sacrificed His life on the cross so that we might have eternal life. This gift, freely given from God's only begotten Son, is the priceless possession of everyone who accepts Him as Lord and Savior. We return our Savior's love by welcoming Him into our hearts and sharing His message and His love. When we do so, we are blessed here on earth and throughout all eternity.

God is the giver, and we are the receivers.
And His richest gifts are bestowed not upon
those who do the greatest things,
but upon those who accept
His abundance and His grace.

Hannah Whitall Smith

God's grace and power seem to reach their peak when we are at our weakest point.

Anne Graham Lotz

We will never cease to need our Father—His wisdom, direction, help, and support. We will never outgrow Him. We will always need His grace.

Kay Arthur

A prayerful heart and an obedient heart will learn, very slowly and not without sorrow, to stake everything on God Himself.

Elisabeth Elliot

The Lord's chief desire is to reveal Himself to you and, in order for Him to do that, He gives you abundant grace. The Lord gives you the experience of enjoying His presence. He touches you, and His touch is so delightful that, more than ever, you are drawn inwardly to Him.

Madame Jeanne Guyon

There is no secret that can separate you from God's love; there is no secret that can separate you from His blessings; there is no secret that is worth keeping from His grace.

Serita Ann Jakes

11

MORE FROM GOD'S WORD

But God, who is abundant in mercy, because of His great love that He had for us, made us alive with the Messiah even though we were dead in trespasses. By grace you are saved!

Ephesians 2:4-5 HCSB

My grace is sufficient for you, for My strength is made perfect in weakness.

2 Corinthians 12:9 NKJV

For by grace you are saved through faith, and this is not from yourselves; it is God's gift—not from works, so that no one can boast.

Ephesians 2:8-9 HCSB

Therefore, since we are receiving a kingdom that cannot be shaken, let us hold on to grace. By it, we may serve God acceptably, with reverence and awe.

Hebrews 12:28 HCSB

The Lord is gracious and compassionate, slow to anger and great in faithful love. The Lord is good to everyone; His compassion [rests] on all He has made.

Psalm 145:8-9 HCSB

For the Lord is good; His mercy is everlasting,
and His truth endures to all generations.

Psalm 100:5 NKJV

SHADES OF GRACE

Number one, God brought me here. It is by His will that I am in this place. In that fact I will rest. Number two, He will keep me here in His love and give me grace to behave as His child. Number three, He will make the trial a blessing, teaching me the lessons He intends for me to learn and working in me the grace He means to bestow. Number four, in His good time He can bring me out again. How and when, He knows. So, let me say I am here.

Andrew Murray

A PRAYER FOR TODAY

Dear Lord, You have offered Your grace freely through Christ Jesus. I praise You for that priceless gift. Let me share the good news of Your Son with a world that desperately needs His peace, His abundance, His love, and His salvation. Amen

Experiencing Christ's Love

For I am persuaded that neither death nor life, nor angels nor principalities nor powers, nor things present nor things to come, nor height nor depth, nor any other created thing, shall be able to separate us from the love of God which is in Christ Jesus our Lord.

Romans 8:38-39 NKJV

How much does Christ love us? More than we, as mere mortals, can comprehend. His love is perfect and steadfast. Even though we are fallible and wayward, the Good Shepherd cares for us still. Even though we have fallen far short of the Father's commandments, Christ loves us with a power and depth that are beyond our understanding. The sacrifice that Jesus made upon the cross was made for each of us, and His love endures to the edge of eternity and beyond.

Christ is the ultimate Savior of mankind and the personal Savior of those who believe in Him. As His servants, we should place Him at the very center of our lives. And, every day that God gives us breath, we should share Christ's love and His message with a world that needs both.

Christ's love changes everything. When you accept His gift of grace, you are transformed, not only for today, but also for all eternity. If you haven't already done so, accept Jesus Christ as your Savior. He's waiting patiently for you to invite Him into your heart. Please don't make Him wait a single minute longer.

It is when we come to the Lord
in our nothingness, our powerlessness and
our helplessness that He then enables us
to love in a way which, without Him,
would be absolutely impossible.

Elisabeth Elliot

The love of Christ is a fierce thing. It can take the picture you have of yourself and burn it in the fire of His loving eyes, replacing it with a true masterpiece.

Sheila Walsh

Live your lives in love, the same sort of love which Christ gives us, and which He perfectly expressed when He gave Himself as a sacrifice to God.

Corrie ten Boom

Blessed assurance, Jesus is mine! O what a foretaste of glory divine!

Fanny Crosby

Christ is with us, and the warmth is contagious.

Joni Eareckson Tada

To a world that was spiritually dry and populated with parched lives scorched by sin, Jesus was the Living Water who would quench the thirsty soul, saving it from "bondage" and filling it with satisfaction and joy and purpose and meaning.

Anne Graham Lotz

When we are in a situation where Jesus is all we have, we soon discover He is all we really need.

Gigi Graham Tchividjian

MORE FROM GOD'S WORD

I am the good shepherd. The good shepherd lays down his life for the sheep.

John 10:11 HCSB

But God proves His own love for us in that while we were still sinners Christ died for us!

Romans 5:8 HCSB

No one has greater love than this, that someone would lay down his life for his friends.

John 15:13 HCSB

Who can separate us from the love of Christ? Can affliction or anguish or persecution or famine or nakedness or danger or sword? . . . No, in all these things we are more than victorious through Him who loved us.

Romans 8:35,37 HCSB

Just as the Father has loved Me, I also have loved you. Remain in My love.

John 15:9 HCSB

If anyone thirsts, let him come to Me and drink.

John 7:37 NKJV

In this world you will have trouble.
But take heart!
I have overcome the world.

John 16:33 NIV

SHADES OF GRACE

It is because of God's loving grace that Jesus died on the cross for our sins so we could experience an eternal relationship with Him.

Bill Bright

A PRAYER FOR TODAY

Dear Jesus, I praise You for Your Love, a love that never ends. Today, I will return Your love and I will share it with the world. Amen

Praise Him and Thank Him

Our prayers for you are always spilling over into thanksgivings. We can't quit thanking God our Father and Jesus our Messiah for you!

Colossians 1:3 MSG

Sometimes, life can be complicated, demanding, and busy. When the demands of life leave us rushing from place to place with scarcely a moment to spare, we may fail to pause and say a word of thanks for all the good things we've received. But when we fail to count our blessings, we rob ourselves of the happiness, the peace, and the gratitude that should rightfully be ours.

Today, even if you're busily engaged in life, slow down long enough to start counting your blessings. You most certainly will not be able to count them all, but take a few moments to jot down as many blessings as you can. Then, give thanks to the Giver of all good things: God. His love for you is eternal, as are His gifts. And it's never too soon—or too late—to offer Him thanks.

The best way to show my gratitude to God is to accept everything, even my problems, with joy.

Mother Teresa

The act of thanksgiving is a demonstration of the fact that you are going to trust and believe God.

Kay Arthur

The game was to just find something about everything to be glad about—no matter what it was. You see, when you're hunting for the glad things, you sort of forget the other kind.

Eleanor H. Porter

God is worthy of our praise and is pleased when we come before Him with thanksgiving.

Shirley Dobson

God has promised that if we harvest well with the tools of thanksgiving, there will be seeds for planting in the spring.

Gloria Gaither

More from God's Word

Thanks be to God for His indescribable gift.

2 Corinthians 9:15 HCSB

Therefore as you have received Christ Jesus the Lord, walk in Him, rooted and built up in Him and established in the faith, just as you were taught, and overflowing with thankfulness.

Colossians 2:6-7 HCSB

Enter into His gates with thanksgiving, and into His courts with praise. Be thankful to Him, and bless His name. For the Lord is good; His mercy is everlasting, and His truth endures to all generations.

Psalm 100:4-5 NKJV

And whatever you do, in word or in deed, do everything in the name of the Lord Jesus, giving thanks to God the Father through Him.

Colossians 3:17 HCSB

I will thank you, Lord, with all my heart; I will tell of all the marvelous things you have done. I will be filled with joy because of you. I will sing praises to your name, O Most High.

Psalm 9:1-2 NLT

And those who have reason to be thankful
should continually sing praises to the Lord.
James 5:13 NLT

SHADES OF GRACE

Grace and gratitude belong together like heaven and earth. Grace evokes gratitude like the voice of an echo. Gratitude follows grace as thunder follows lightning.

Karl Barth

A PRAYER FOR TODAY

Heavenly Father, Your gifts are greater than I can imagine. May I live each day with thanksgiving in my heart and praise on my lips. Thank You for the gift of Your Son and for the promise of eternal life. Let me share the joyous news of Jesus Christ, and let my life be a testimony to His love and His grace. Amen

Serve Him

We know we love God's children if we love God and obey his commandments.

1 John 5:2 NLT

The teachings of Jesus are clear: We achieve greatness through service to others. But, as weak human beings, we sometimes fall short as we seek to puff ourselves up and glorify our own accomplishments. Jesus commands otherwise. He teaches us that the most esteemed men and women are not the self-congratulatory leaders of society but are instead the humblest of servants.

Today, you may feel the temptation to build yourself up in the eyes of your neighbors. Resist that temptation. Instead, serve your neighbors quietly and without fanfare. Find a need and fill it...humbly. Lend a helping hand and share a word of kindness...anonymously, for this is God's way.

As a humble servant, you will glorify yourself not before men, but before God, and that's what God intends. After all, earthly glory is fleeting: here today and all too soon gone. But, heavenly glory endures throughout eternity. So, the choice is yours: Either you can lift yourself up here on earth and be humbled in heaven, or vice versa. Choose vice versa.

If you want to discover your spiritual gifts, start obeying God. As you serve Him, you will find that He has given you the gifts that are necessary to follow through in obedience.

Anne Graham Lotz

We can love Jesus in the hungry, the naked, and the destitute who are dying…If you love, you will be willing to serve. And you will find Jesus in the distressing disguise of the poor.

Mother Teresa

Doing something positive toward another person is a practical approach to feeling good about yourself.

Barbara Johnson

God wants us to serve Him with a willing spirit, one that would choose no other way.

Beth Moore

In the very place where God has put us, whatever its limitations, whatever kind of work it may be, we may indeed serve the Lord Christ.

Elisabeth Elliot

I am more and more persuaded that all that is required of us is faithful seed-sowing. The harvest is bound to follow.

Annie Armstrong

MORE FROM GOD'S WORD

Worship the Lord your God and . . . serve Him only.

Matthew 4:10 HCSB

A person should consider us in this way: as servants of Christ and managers of God's mysteries. In this regard, it is expected of managers that each one be found faithful.

1 Corinthians 4:1-2 HCSB

If they serve Him obediently, they will end their days in prosperity and their years in happiness.

Job 36:11 HCSB

We must do the works of Him who sent Me while it is day. Night is coming when no one can work.

John 9:4 HCSB

Serve the Lord with gladness.

Psalm 100:2 HCSB

The greatest among you will be your servant. For whoever exalts himself will be humbled, and whoever humbles himself will be exalted.

Matthew 23:11-12 NIV

Never be lacking in zeal,
but keep your spiritual fervor, serving the Lord.

Romans 12:11 NIV

SHADES OF GRACE

Kindness in this world will do much to help others, not only to come into the light, but also to grow in grace day by day.

Fanny Crosby

A PRAYER FOR TODAY

Dear Lord, in weak moments, I seek to build myself up by placing myself ahead of others. But Your commandment, Father, is that I become a humble servant to those who need my encouragement, my help, and my love. Create in me a servant's heart. And, let me be a woman who follows in the footsteps of Your Son Jesus who taught us by example that to be great in Your eyes, Lord, is to serve others humbly, faithfully, and lovingly. Amen

Finding Genuine Peace

But now in Christ Jesus you who once were far off have been brought near by the blood of Christ. For He Himself is our peace.

Ephesians 2:13-14 NKJV

On many occasions, our outer struggles are simply manifestations of the inner conflicts that we feel when we stray from God's path. What's needed is a refresher course in God's promise of peace. The beautiful words of John 14:27 remind us that Jesus offers peace, not as the world gives, but as He alone gives: "Peace I leave with you. My peace I give to you. I do not give to you as the world gives. Your heart must not be troubled or fearful" (HCSB).

As believers, our challenge is straightforward: we should welcome Christ's peace into our hearts and then, as best we can, share His peace with others.

Today, as a gift to yourself, to your family, and to your friends, invite Christ to preside over every aspect of your life. It's the best way to live and the surest path to peace . . . today and forever.

To know God as He really is—in His essential nature and character—is to arrive at a citadel of peace that circumstances may storm, but can never capture.

Catherine Marshall

In the center of a hurricane there is
absolute quiet and peace.
There is no safer place than
in the center of the will of God.

Corrie ten Boom

I believe that in every time and place it is within our power to acquiesce in the will of God—and what peace it brings to do so!

Elisabeth Elliot

I want first of all…to be at peace with myself. I want a singleness of eye, a purity of intention, a central core to my life…. I want, in fact—to borrow from the language of the saints—to live "in grace" as much of the time as possible.

Anne Morrow Lindbergh

When we do what is right, we have contentment, peace, and happiness.

Beverly LaHaye

Prayer guards hearts and minds and causes God to bring peace out of chaos.

Beth Moore

Every one of us is supposed to be a powerhouse for God, living in balance and harmony within and without.

Joyce Meyer

 Where the soul is full of peace and joy, outward surroundings and circumstances are of comparatively little account.

Hannah Whitall Smiith

The Holy Spirit testifies of Jesus. So when you are filled with the Holy Spirit you speak about our Lord and really live to His honor.

Corrie ten Boom

MORE FROM GOD'S WORD

If it is possible, as far as it depends on you, live at peace with everyone.

Romans 12:18 NIV

And the peace of God, which surpasses all understanding, will guard your hearts and minds through Christ Jesus. Finally, brethren, whatever things are true, whatever things are noble, whatever things are just, whatever things are pure, whatever things are lovely, whatever things are of good report, if there is any virtue and if there is anything praiseworthy—meditate on these things.

Philippians 4:7-8 NKJV

Blessed are the peacemakers, for they will be called sons of God.

Matthew 5:9 NIV

A heart at peace gives life to the body, but envy rots the bones.

Proverbs 14:30 NIV

The LORD gives strength to his people;
the LORD blesses his people with peace.

Psalm 29:11 NIV

SHADES OF GRACE

All men who live with any degree of serenity
live by some assurance of grace.

Reinhold Niebuhr

A PRAYER FOR TODAY

Dear Lord, let me accept the peace and abundance that
You offer through Your Son Jesus. You are the Giver of all
things good, Father, and You give me peace when I draw
close to You. Help me to trust Your will, to follow Your
commands, and to accept Your peace, today and forever.
Amen

His Grace Is Sufficient for Difficult Days

We are troubled on every side, yet not distressed; we are perplexed, but not in despair....

2 Corinthians 4:8 KJV

As we travel the roads of life, all of us are confronted with streets that seem to be dead ends. When we do, we may become discouraged. After all, we live in a society where expectations can be high and demands even higher.

If you find yourself enduring difficult circumstances, remember that God remains in His heaven. If you become discouraged with the direction of your day or your life, turn your thoughts and prayers to Him. He is a God of possibility, not negativity. He will guide you through your difficulties and beyond them. And then, with a renewed spirit of optimism and hope, you can thank the Giver of all things good for gifts that are simply too profound to fully understand and for treasures that are too numerous to count.

If God sends us on stony paths, He provides strong shoes.

Corrie ten Boom

Often God shuts a door in our face
so that He can open the door through which
He wants us to go.

Catherine Marshall

This hard place in which you perhaps find yourself is the very place in which God is giving you opportunity to look only to Him, to spend time in prayer, and to learn long-suffering, gentleness, meekness—in short, to learn the depths of the love that Christ Himself has poured out on all of us.

Elisabeth Elliot

We all go through pain and sorrow, but the presence of God, like a warm, comforting blanket, can shield us and protect us, and allow the deep inner joy to surface, even in the most devastating circumstances.

Barbara Johnson

Often the trials we mourn are really gateways into the good things we long for.

Hannah Whitall Smith

Recently I've been learning that life comes down to this: God is in everything. Regardless of what difficulties I am experiencing at the moment, or what things aren't as I would like them to be, I look at the circumstances and say, "Lord, what are you trying to teach me?"

Catherine Marshall

Worries carry responsibilities that belong to God, not to you. Worry does not enable us to escape evil; it makes us unfit to cope with it when it comes.

Corrie ten Boom

God will never let you sink under your circumstances. He always provides a safety net and His love always encircles.

Barbara Johnson

Whether our fear is absolutely realistic or out of proportion in our minds, our greatest refuge is Jesus Christ.

Luci Swindoll

MORE FROM GOD'S WORD

We also have joy with our troubles, because we know that these troubles produce patience. And patience produces character, and character produces hope.

Romans 5:3-4 NCV

The LORD also will be a stronghold for the oppressed, a stronghold in times of trouble.

Psalm 9:9 NASB

You pulled me from the brink of death, my feet from the cliff-edge of doom. Now I stroll at leisure with God in the sunlit fields of life.

Psalm 56:13 MSG

Come to Me, all you who labor and are heavy laden, and I will give you rest. Take My yoke upon you and learn from Me, for I am gentle and lowly in heart, and you will find rest for your souls. For My yoke is easy and My burden is light.

Matthew 11:28-30 NKJV

The Lord is the One who will go before you. He will be with you; He will not leave you or forsake you. Do not be afraid or discouraged.

Deuteronomy 31:8 HCSB

For God has not given us a spirit of fear, but of power and of love and of a sound mind.

2 Timothy 1:7 NKJV

SHADES OF GRACE

Grace grows best in the winter.

C. H. Spurgeon

A PRAYER FOR TODAY

Heavenly Father, You are my strength and my refuge. As I journey through this day, I know that I may encounter disappointments and losses. When I am troubled, let me turn to You. Keep me steady, Lord, and renew a right spirit inside of me this day and forever. Amen

Dreaming Big Dreams

When dreams come true, there is life and joy.

Proverbs 13:12 NLT

Are you willing to entertain the possibility that God has big plans in store for you? Hopefully so. Yet sometimes, especially if you've recently experienced a life-altering disappointment, you may find it difficult to envision a brighter future for yourself and your family. If so, it's time to reconsider your own capabilities . . . and God's.

Your Heavenly Father created you with unique gifts and untapped talents; your job is to tap them. When you do, you'll begin to feel an increasing sense of confidence in yourself and in your future.

It takes courage to dream big dreams. You will discover that courage when you do three things: accept the past, trust God to handle the future, and make the most of the time He has given you today.

Nothing is too difficult for God, and no dreams are too big for Him—not even yours. So start living—and dreaming—accordingly.

The future belongs to those who believe in the beauty of their dreams.

Eleanor Roosevelt

The future lies all before us. Shall it only be a slight advance upon what we usually do? Ought it not to be a bound, a leap forward to altitudes of endeavor and success undreamed of before?

Annie Armstrong

Never be afraid to trust an unknown future
to a known God.

Corrie ten Boom

You pay God a compliment by asking great things of Him.

St. Teresa of Avila

Our dreams are who we are.

Barbara Sher

39

Always stay connected to people and seek out things that bring you joy. Dream with abandon. Pray confidently.

Barbara Johnson

God created us with an overwhelming desire to soar. He designed us to be tremendously productive and "to mount up with wings like eagles," realistically dreaming of what He can do with our potential.

Carol Kent

Allow your dreams a place in your prayers and plans. God-given dreams can help you move into the future He is preparing for you.

Barbara Johnson

Forgetting your mission leads, inevitably, to getting tangled up in details—details that can take you completely off your path.

Laurie Beth Jones

MORE FROM GOD'S WORD

Live full lives, full in the fullness of God. God can do anything, you know—far more than you could ever imagine or guess or request in your wildest dreams! He does it not by pushing us around but by working within us, his Spirit deeply and gently within us.

Ephesians 3:19-20 MSG

I came so they can have real and eternal life, more and better life than they ever dreamed of.

John 10:10 MSG

It is pleasant to see dreams come true, but fools will not turn from evil to attain them.

Proverbs 13:19 NLT

Where there is no vision, the people perish....

Proverbs 29:18 KJV

Be of good courage, and he shall strengthen your heart, all ye that hope in the LORD.

Psalm 31:24 KJV

41

There is surely a future hope for you,
and your hope will not be cut off.

Proverbs 23:18 NIV

SHADES OF GRACE

Grace calls you to get up, throw off your blanket of helplessness, and to move on through life in faith.

Kay Arthur

A PRAYER FOR TODAY

Dear Lord, give me the courage to dream and the faithfulness to trust in Your perfect plan. When I am worried or weary, give me strength for today and hope for tomorrow. Keep me mindful of Your healing power, Your infinite love, and Your eternal salvation. Amen

Praise Him for Your Talents

God has given gifts to each of you from his great variety of spiritual gifts. Manage them well so that God's generosity can flow through you.

1 Peter 4:10 NLT

Your talents, resources, and opportunities are all gifts from the Giver of all things good. And the best way to say "Thank You" for these gifts is to use them.

Do you have a particular talent? Hone your skill and use it. Do you possess financial resources? Share them. Have you been blessed by a particular opportunity, or have you experienced unusual good fortune? Use your good fortune to help others.

When you share the gifts God has given you—and when you share them freely and without fanfare—you invite God to bless you more and more. So today, do yourself and the world a favor: be a faithful steward of your talents and treasures. And then prepare yourself for even greater blessings that are sure to come.

The Lord has abundantly blessed me all of my life. I'm not trying to pay Him back for all of His wonderful gifts; I just realize that He gave them to me to give away.

Lisa Whelchel

You can't climb the ladder of life with your hands in your pockets.

Barbara Johnson

God never calls without enabling us. In other words, if He calls you to do something, He makes it possible for you to do it.

Luci Swindoll

What we are is God's gift to us. What we become is our gift to God.

Anonymous

God has given you special talents—now it's your turn to give them back to God.

Marie T. Freeman

Not everyone possesses boundless energy or a conspicuous talent. We are not equally blessed with great intellect or physical beauty or emotional strength. But we have all been given the same ability to be faithful.

Gigi Graham Tchividjian

It is the definition of joy to be able to offer back to God the essence of what He's placed in you, be that creativity or a love of ideas or a compassionate heart or the gift of hospitality.

Paula Rinehart

Yes, we need to acknowledge our weaknesses, to confess our sins. But if we want to be active, productive participants in the realm of God, we also need to recognize our gifts, to appreciate our strengths, to build on the abilities God has given us. We need to balance humility with confidence.

Penelope Stokes

Great relief and satisfaction can come from seeking God's priorities for us in each season, discerning what is "best" in the midst of many noble opportunities, and pouring our most excellent energies into those things.

Beth Moore

45

More from God's Word

According to the grace given to us, we have different gifts: If prophecy, use it according to the standard of faith; if service, in service; if teaching, in teaching; if exhorting, in exhortation; giving, with generosity; leading, with diligence; showing mercy, with cheerfulness.

Romans 12:6-8 HCSB

Do not neglect the gift that is in you.

1 Timothy 4:14 HCSB

Each one has his own gift from God, one in this manner and another in that.

1 Corinthians 7:7 NKJV

So he who had received five talents came and brought five other talents, saying, "Lord, you delivered to me five talents; look, I have gained five more talents besides them." His lord said to him, "Well done, good and faithful servant; you were faithful over a few things, I will make you ruler over many things. Enter into the joy of your lord."

Matthew 25:20-21 NKJV

*I remind you to keep ablaze the gift of God
that is in you.*

2 Timothy 1:6 HCSB

SHADES OF GRACE

When you experience grace and are loved when
you do not deserve it, you spend the rest of your
life standing on tiptoes trying to reach His plan
for your life out of gratitude.

Charles Stanley

A PRAYER FOR TODAY

*Father, You have given me abilities to be used for the
glory of Your kingdom. Give me the courage and the
perseverance to use those talents. Keep me mindful that
all my gifts come from You, Lord. Let me be Your faithful,
humble servant, and let me give You all the glory and all
the praise. Amen*

Trusting Your Conscience

I will maintain my righteousness and never let go of it; my conscience will not reproach me as long as I live.

Job 27:6 NIV

Few things in life torment us more than a guilty conscience. And, few things in life provide more contentment than the knowledge that we are obeying God's commandments. A clear conscience is one of the rewards we earn when we obey God's Word and follow His will. When we follow God's will and accept His gift of salvation, our earthly rewards are never-ceasing, and our heavenly rewards are everlasting.

Billy Graham correctly observed, "Most of us follow our conscience as we follow a wheelbarrow. We push it in front of us in the direction we want to go." If that describes you, then here's a word of warning: both you and your wheelbarrow are headed for trouble.

You can sometimes keep secrets from other people, but you can never keep secrets from God. God knows what you think and what you do. And if you want to please Him, you must start with good intentions, a pure heart, and a clear conscience.

If you sincerely wish to walk with God, follow His commandments. When you do, your character will take care of itself...and so will your conscience. Then, as you journey through life, you won't need to look over your shoulder to see who—besides God—is watching.

God desires that we become spiritually
healthy enough through faith to have
a conscience that rightly interprets
the work of the Holy Spirit.

Beth Moore

If you listen to your conscience, it will serve you as no other friend you'll ever know.

Loretta Young

Let us never suppose that obedience is impossible or that holiness is meant only for a select few. Our Shepherd leads us in paths of righteousness—not for our name's sake but for His.

Elisabeth Elliot

If I am walking along the street with a very disfiguring hole in the back of my dress, of which I am in ignorance, it is certainly a very great comfort to me to have a kind friend who will tell me of it. And similarly, it is indeed a comfort to know that there is always abiding with me a divine, all-seeing Comforter, who will reprove me for all my faults and will not let me go on in a fatal unconsciousness of them.

Hannah Whitall Smith

While conscience is our friend, all is at peace; however once it is offended, farewell to a tranquil mind.

Lady Mary Wortley Montagu

Whatever weakens your reason, impairs the tenderness of your conscience, obscures your sense of God, or removes your relish for spiritual things—that is sin to you.

Susanna Wesley

There is a balance to be maintained in situations. That balance is the Holy Spirit within us to guide us into the truth of each situation and circumstance in which we find ourselves. He will provide us the wisdom to know when we are to be adaptable and adjustable and when we are to take a firm stand and be immovable.

Joyce Meyer

Jesus is Victor. Calvary is the place of victory. Obedience is the pathway of victory. Bible study and prayer is the preparation for victory.

Corrie ten Boom

When we do what is right, we have contentment, peace, and happiness.

Beverly LaHaye

MORE FROM GOD'S WORD

So I strive always to keep my conscience clear before God and man.

Acts 24:16 NIV

Let us draw near to God with a sincere heart in full assurance of faith, having our hearts sprinkled to cleanse us from a guilty conscience and having our bodies washed with pure water.

Hebrews 10:22 NIV

Now the goal of our instruction is love from a pure heart, a good conscience, and a sincere faith.

1 Timothy 1:5 HCSB

Therefore whoever hears these sayings of Mine, and does them, I will liken him to a wise man who built his house on the rock: and the rain descended, the floods came, and the winds blew and beat on that house; and it did not fall, for it was founded on the rock.

Matthew 7:24-25 NKJV

Create in me a pure heart, O God,
and renew a steadfast spirit within me.
Psalm 51:10 NIV

SHADES OF GRACE

Grace is not about finishing last or first; it is about not counting. We receive grace as a gift from God, not as something we toil to earn.

Philip Yancey

A PRAYER FOR TODAY

Dear Lord, You speak to me through the gift of Your Holy Word. And, Father, You speak to me through that still small voice that tells me right from wrong. Let me follow Your way, Lord, and, in these quiet moments, show me Your plan for this day, that I might serve You. Amen

Finding Contentment

But godliness with contentment is a great gain.

1 Timothy 6:6 HCSB

Everywhere we turn, or so it seems, the world promises us contentment and happiness. We are bombarded by messages offering us the "good life" if only we will purchase products and services that are designed to provide happiness, success, and contentment. But the contentment that the world offers is fleeting and incomplete. Thankfully, the contentment that God offers is all encompassing and everlasting.

Happiness depends less upon our circumstances than upon our thoughts. When we turn our thoughts to God, to His gifts, and to His glorious creation, we experience the joy that God intends for His children. But, when we focus on the negative aspects of life— or when we disobey God's commandments—we cause ourselves needless suffering.

Do you sincerely want to be a contented Christian? Then set your mind and your heart upon God's love and His grace. Seek first the salvation that is available through a personal relationship with Jesus Christ, and then claim the joy, the contentment, and the spiritual abundance that God offers His children.

When you accept rather than fight
your circumstances, even though
you don't understand them,
you open your heart's gate to God's love,
peace, joy, and contentment.

Amy Carmichael

Oh, what a happy soul I am, although I cannot see!
I am resolved that in this world, contented I will be.

Fanny Crosby

If I could just hang in there, being faithful to my own
tasks, God would make me joyful and content. The
responsibility is mine, but the power is His.

Peg Rankin

The key to contentment is to consider. Consider who
you are and be satisfied with that. Consider what you
have and be satisfied with that. Consider what God's
doing and be satisfied with that.

Luci Swindoll

Jesus Christ is the One by Whom, for Whom, through
Whom everything was made. Therefore, He knows
what's wrong in your life and how to fix it.

Anne Graham Lotz

God is everything that is good and comfortable for us.
He is our clothing that for love wraps us, clasps us, and
all surrounds us for tender love.

Juliana of Norwich

MORE FROM GOD'S WORD

A tranquil heart is life to the body, but jealousy is rottenness to the bones.

Proverbs 14:30 HCSB

How priceless is your unfailing love! Both high and low among men find refuge in the shadow of your wings. They feast on the abundance of your house; you give them drink from your river of delights. For with you is the fountain of life; in your light we see light.

Psalm 36:7-9 NIV

Let your conduct be without covetousness; be content with such things as you have. For He Himself has said, "I will never leave you nor forsake you."

Hebrews 13:5 NKJV

For the happy heart, life is a continual feast.

Proverbs 15:15 NLT

How happy are those whose way is blameless, who live according to the law of the Lord! Happy are those who keep His decrees and seek Him with all their heart.

Psalm 119:1-2 HCSB

*I have learned to be content in whatever
circumstances I am.*

Philippians 4:11 HCSB

SHADES OF GRACE

How beautiful it is to learn that grace isn't fragile, and that in the family of God we can fail and not be a failure.

Gloria Gaither

A PRAYER FOR TODAY

Dear Lord, You offer me contentment, and I praise You for that gift. Today, I will accept Your peace. I will trust Your Word, I will follow Your commandments, and I will welcome the peace of Jesus into my heart, today and forever. Amen

Trust His Promises

This is my comfort in my affliction: Your promise has given me life.

Psalm 119:50 HCSB

God's promises are found in a book like no other: the Holy Bible. It is a roadmap for life here on earth and for life eternal. As Christians, we are called upon to trust its promises, to follow its commandments, and to share its Good News.

As believers, we must study the Bible daily and meditate upon its meaning for our lives. Otherwise, we deprive ourselves of a priceless gift from our Creator. God's Holy Word is, indeed, a transforming, life-changing, one-of-a-kind treasure. And, a passing acquaintance with the Good Book is insufficient for Christians who seek to obey God's Word and to understand His will.

God has made promises to mankind and to you. God's promises never fail and they never grow old. You must trust those promises and share them with your family, with your friends, and with the world.

Joy is not mere happiness. Nor does joy spring from a life of ease, comfort, or peaceful circumstances. Joy is the soul's buoyant response to a God of promise, presence, and power.

Susan Lenzkes

Claim all of God's promises in the Bible.
Your sins, your worries, your life—
you may cast them all on Him.

Corrie ten Boom

We have ample evidence that the Lord is able to guide. The promises cover every imaginable situation. All we need to do is to take the hand He stretches out.

Elisabeth Elliot

Do not be afraid, then, that if you trust, or tell others to trust, the matter will end there. Trust is only the beginning and the continual foundation. When we trust Him, the Lord works, and His work is the important part of the whole matter.

Hannah Whitall Smith

Brother, is your faith looking upward today? / Trust in the promise of the Savior. / Sister, is the light shining bright on your way? / Trust in the promise of thy Lord.

Fanny Crosby

The meaning of hope isn't just some flimsy wishing. It's a firm confidence in God's promises—that He will ultimately set things right.

Sheila Walsh

Fear and doubt are conquered by a faith that rejoices. And faith can rejoice because the promises of God are as certain as God Himself.

Kay Arthur

For Christians who believe God's promises, the future is actually too bright to comprehend.

Marie T. Freeman

The love of God is so vast, the power of His touch so invigorating, we could just stay in His presence for hours, soaking up His glory, basking in His blessings.

Debra Evans

MORE FROM GOD'S WORD

Whatever God has promised gets stamped with the Yes of Jesus. In him, this is what we preach and pray, the great Amen, God's Yes and our Yes together, gloriously evident.

2 Corinthians 1:20 MSG

Let's keep a firm grip on the promises that keep us going. He always keeps his word.

Hebrews 10:23 MSG

For ye have need of patience, that, after ye have done the will of God, ye might receive the promise.

Hebrews 10:36 KJV

And we desire that each one of you show the same diligence so as to realize the full assurance of hope until the end, so that you will not be sluggish, but imitators of those who through faith and patience inherit the promises.

Hebrews 6:11-12 NASB

You will be a good servant of Christ Jesus, nourished by the words of the faith and of the good teaching that you have followed.

1 Timothy 4:6 HCSB

*Man shall not live by bread alone,
but by every word that proceeds
from the mouth of God.*

Matthew 4:4 NKJV

SHADES OF GRACE

Grace comes from the heart of a gracious God who wants to stun you and overwhelm you with a gift you don't deserve—salvation, adoption, a spiritual ability to use in kingdom service, answered prayer, the church, His presence, His wisdom, His guidance, His love.

Bill Hybels

A PRAYER FOR TODAY

Lord, Your Holy Word contains promises, and I will trust them. I will use the Bible as my guide, and I will trust You, Lord, to speak to me through Your Holy Spirit and through Your Holy Word, this day and forever. Amen

Spiritual Growth

Grow in grace and understanding of our Master and Savior, Jesus Christ. Glory to the Master, now and forever! Yes!

2 Peter 3:18 MSG

Are you continuing to grow in your love and knowledge of the Lord, or are you "satisfied" with the current state of your spiritual health? Your relationship with God is ongoing; it unfolds day by day, and it offers countless opportunities to grow closer to Him . . . or not. As each new day unfolds, you are confronted with a wide range of decisions: how you will behave, where you will direct your thoughts, with whom you will associate, and what you will choose to worship. These choices, along with many others like them, are yours and yours alone. How you choose determines how your relationship with God will unfold.

Hopefully, you're determined to make yourself a growing Christian. Your Savior deserves no less, and neither, by the way, do you.

Growing up in Christ is surely the most difficult, courageous, exhilarating, and eternally important work any of us will ever do.

Susan Lenzkes

You are either becoming more like Christ every day or you're becoming less like Him. There is no neutral position in the Lord.

Stormie Omartian

There is nothing more important than understanding God's truth and being changed by it, so why are we so casual about accepting the popular theology of the moment without checking it out for ourselves? God has given us a mind so that we can learn and grow. As His people, we have a great responsibility and wonderful privilege of growing in our understanding of Him.

Sheila Walsh

If all struggles and sufferings were eliminated, the spirit would no more reach maturity than would the child.

Elisabeth Elliot

Maturity in Christ is about consistent pursuit in spite of the attacks and setbacks. It is about remaining in the arms of God. Abiding and staying, even in my weakness, even in my failure.

Angela Thomas

Suffering is never for nothing. It is that you and I might be conformed to the image of Christ.

Elisabeth Elliot

We set our eyes on the finish line, forgetting the past, and straining toward the mark of spiritual maturity and fruitfulness.

Vonette Bright

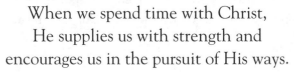

When we spend time with Christ, He supplies us with strength and encourages us in the pursuit of His ways.

Elizabeth George

"They that sow bountifully shall reap also bountifully," is as true in spiritual things as in material.

Lottie Moon

MORE FROM GOD'S WORD

For this reason also, since the day we heard this, we haven't stopped praying for you. We are asking that you may be filled with the knowledge of His will in all wisdom and spiritual understanding.

Colossians 1:9 HCSB

I want their hearts to be encouraged and joined together in love, so that they may have all the riches of assured understanding, and have the knowledge of God's mystery—Christ.

Colossians 2:2 HCSB

Therefore, leaving the elementary message about the Messiah, let us go on to maturity.

Hebrews 6:1 HCSB

For You, O God, have tested us; You have refined us as silver is refined. You brought us into the net; You laid affliction on our backs. You have caused men to ride over our heads; we went through fire and through water; but You brought us out to rich fulfillment.

Psalm 66:10–12 NKJV

Run away from infantile indulgence.
Run after mature righteousness—
faith, love, peace—joining those who are
in honest and serious prayer before God.
2 Timothy 2:22 MSG

SHADES OF GRACE

We shall grow in grace, but we shall never be more completely pardoned than the moment we first believed.

C. H. Spurgeon

A PRAYER FOR TODAY

Dear Lord, thank You for the opportunity to walk with Your Son. And, thank You for the opportunity to grow closer to You each day. I thank You for the person I am . . . and for the person I can become. Amen

Strength for Today

Search for the Lord and for His strength; seek His face always.

Psalm 105:4-5 HCSB

God's love and support never changes. From the cradle to the grave, God has promised to give you the strength to meet any challenge. God has promised to lift you up and guide your steps if you let Him. God has promised that when you entrust your life to Him completely and without reservation, He will give you the courage to face any trial and the wisdom to live in His righteousness.

God's hand uplifts those who turn their hearts and prayers to Him. Will you count yourself among that number? Will you accept God's peace and wear God's armor against the temptations and distractions of our dangerous world? If you do, you can live courageously and optimistically, knowing that you have been forever touched by the loving, unfailing, uplifting hand of God.

The miraculous thing about being a family is that in the last analysis, we are each dependent of one another and God, woven together by mercy given and mercy received.

Barbara Johnson

No matter how heavy the burden, daily strength is given, so I expect we need not give ourselves any concern as to what the outcome will be. We must simply go forward.

Annie Armstrong

If we just give God the little that we have,
we can trust Him to make it go around.

Gloria Gaither

If your every human plan and calculation has miscarried, if, one by one, human props have been knocked out...take heart. God is trying to get a message through to you, and the message is: "Stop depending on inadequate human resources. Let me handle the matter."

Catherine Marshall

Living by faith requires patience, for the one who lives by faith becomes dependent upon God.

Kay Arthur

By ourselves we are not capable of suffering bravely, but the Lord possesses all the strength we lack and will demonstrate His power when we undergo persecution.

Corrie ten Boom

From the very moment one feels called to act is born the strength to bear whatever horror one will feel or see. In some inexplicable way, terror loses its overwhelming power when it becomes a task that must be faced.

Emmi Bonhoeffer

When we reach the end of our strength, wisdom, and personal resources, we enter into the beginning of His glorious provisions.

Patsy Clairmont

MORE FROM GOD'S WORD

And He said to me, "My grace is sufficient for you, for My strength is made perfect in weakness."

2 Corinthians 12:9 NKJV

You, therefore, my child, be strong in the grace that is in Christ Jesus.

2 Timothy 2:1 HCSB

The Lord is my strength and my song; He has become my salvation.

Exodus 15:2 HCSB

He gives strength to the weary and strengthens the powerless.

Isaiah 40:29 HCSB

But those who wait on the Lord shall renew their strength; they shall mount up with wings like eagles, they shall run and not be weary, they shall walk and not faint.

Isaiah 40:31 NKJV

I sought the Lord, and He heard me, and delivered me from all my fears.

Psalm 34:4 NKJV

*Even when I walk through the dark valley
of death, I will not be afraid,
for you are close beside me. Your rod and
your staff protect and comfort me.*

Psalm 23:4 NLT

SHADES OF GRACE

God's grace is just the right amount of just the
right quality arriving as if from nowhere at just
the right time.

Bill Bright

A PRAYER FOR TODAY

*Dear Lord, I will turn to You for strength. When my
responsibilities seem overwhelming, I will trust You to give
me courage and perspective. Today and every day, I will
look to You as the ultimate source of my hope, my strength,
my peace, and my salvation. Amen*

Making the Right Decisions

Now if any of you lacks wisdom, he should ask God, who gives to all generously and without criticizing, and it will be given to him.

James 1:5 HCSB

Some decisions are easy to make because the consequences of those decisions are small. When the person behind the counter asks, "Want fries with that?" the necessary response requires little thought because the aftermath of that decision is relatively unimportant.

Some decisions, on the other hand, are big . . . very big. If you're facing one of those big decisions, here are some things you can do: 1. Gather as much information as you can: don't expect to get all the facts—that's impossible—but get as many facts as you can in a reasonable amount of time. (Proverbs 24:3-4) 2. Don't be too impulsive: If you have time to make a decision, use that time to make a good decision. (Proverbs 19:2) 3. Rely on the advice of trusted friends and mentors. Proverbs 1:5 makes it clear: "A wise man will hear and increase learning, and a man of understanding will attain wise counsel" (NKJV). 4. Pray for guidance. When you seek it, He will give it. (Luke 11:9) 5. Trust the quiet inner voice of your conscience: Treat your conscience as you would a trusted advisor. (Luke 17:21) 6. When the time for action arrives, act. Procrastination is the enemy of progress; don't let it defeat you. (James 1:22).

People who can never quite seem to make up their minds usually make themselves miserable. So when in doubt, be decisive. It's the decent way to live.

There may be no trumpet sound or
loud applause when we make
a right decision, just a calm sense of
resolution and peace.

Gloria Gaither

The Reference Point for the Christian is the Bible. All values, judgments, and attitudes must be gauged in relationship to this Reference Point.

Ruth Bell Graham

The principle of making no decision without prayer keeps me from rushing in and committing myself before I consult God.

Elizabeth George

If you are struggling to make some difficult decisions right now that aren't specifically addressed in the Bible, don't make a choice based on what's right for someone else. You are the Lord's and He will make sure you do what's right.

Lisa Whelchel

We cannot be led by our emotions and still be led by the Holy Spirit, so we have to make a choice.

Joyce Meyer

The pathway of obedience can sometimes be difficult, but it always leads to a strengthening of our inner woman.

Vonette Bright

MORE FROM GOD'S WORD

I have set before you life and death, blessing and curse. Choose life so that you and your descendants may live, love the Lord your God, obey Him, and remain faithful to Him. For He is your life, and He will prolong your life in the land the Lord swore to give to your fathers Abraham, Isaac, and Jacob.

Deuteronomy 30:19-20 HCSB

Ignorant zeal is worthless; haste makes waste.

Proverbs 19:2 MSG

But Daniel purposed in his heart that he would not defile himself....

Daniel 1:8 KJV

But seek first the kingdom of God and His righteousness, and all these things will be provided for you.

Matthew 6:33 HCSB

Above all and before all, do this: Get Wisdom! Write this at the top of your list: Get Understanding!

Proverbs 4:7 MSG

The wise people will shine like the brightness of the sky. Those who teach others to live right will shine like stars forever and ever.

Daniel 12:3 NCV

SHADES OF GRACE

The Gospel is not so much a demand as it is an offer, an offer of new life to man by the grace of God.

E. Stanley Jones

A PRAYER FOR TODAY

Dear Lord, today I will focus my thoughts on Your will for my life. I will strive to make decisions that are pleasing to You, and I will strive to follow in the footsteps of Your Son. Amen

Beyond Discouragement

He gives power to the weak, and to those who have no might He increases strength.

Isaiah 40:29 NKJV

We Christians have many reasons to celebrate. God is in His heaven; Christ has risen, and we are the sheep of His flock. Yet sometimes, even the most devout believers may become discouraged. After all, we live in a world where expectations can be high and demands can be even higher.

When we fail to meet the expectations of others (or, for that matter, the expectations that we have for ourselves), we may be tempted to abandon hope. But God has other plans. He knows exactly how He intends to use us. Our task is to remain faithful until He does.

If you're a woman who has become discouraged with the direction of your day or your life, turn your thoughts and prayers to God. He is a God of possibility, not negativity. He will help you count your bless-

ings instead of your hardships. And then, with a renewed spirit of optimism and hope, you can properly
thank your Father in heaven for His blessings, for His
love, and for His Son.

Overcoming discouragement is simply a matter of
taking away the DIS and adding the EN.

Barbara Johnson

Just as courage is faith in good, so discouragement is
faith in evil, and, while courage opens the door to
good, discouragement opens it to evil.

Hannah Whitall Smith

The strength that we claim from God's Word does
not depend on circumstances. Circumstances will be
difficult, but our strength will be sufficient.

Corrie ten Boom

Would we know the major chords were so sweet if
there were no minor key?

Mrs. Charles E. Cowman

MORE FROM GOD'S WORD

But as for you, be strong; don't be discouraged, for your work has a reward.

2 Chronicles 15:7 HCSB

The Lord is the One who will go before you. He will be with you; He will not leave you or forsake you. Do not be afraid or discouraged.

Deuteronomy 31:8 HCSB

In my distress I prayed to the LORD, and the LORD answered me and rescued me. The LORD is for me, so I will not be afraid.

Psalm 118:5-6 NLT

He will not fear bad news; his heart is confident, trusting in the Lord. His heart is assured; he will not fear.

Psalm 112:7-8 HCSB

Don't be afraid. Only believe.

Mark 5:36 HCSB

I sought the Lord, and He answered me and delivered me from all my fears.

Psalm 34:4 HCSB

SHADES OF GRACE

All praise to our redeeming Lord, who joins us by His grace and bids us, each to each restored, together seek His face.

Charles Wesley

A PRAYER FOR TODAY

Dear Lord, when I am discouraged, give me perspective and faith. When I am weak, give me strength. When I am fearful, give me courage for the day ahead. I will trust in Your promises, Father, and I will live with the assurance that You are with me not only for this day, but also throughout all eternity. Amen

Your Own Worst Critic?

A devout life does bring wealth, but it's the rich simplicity of being yourself before God.

1 Timothy 6:6 MSG

A re you your own worst critic? If so, it's time to become a little more understanding of the woman you see whenever you look into the mirror.

Millions of words have been written about various ways to improve self-image and increase self-esteem. Yet, maintaining a healthy self-image is, to a surprising extent, a matter of doing three things: 1. behaving ourselves 2. thinking healthy thoughts 3. finding a purpose for your life that pleases your Creator and yourself.

The Bible affirms the importance of self-acceptance by teaching Christians to love others as they love themselves (Matthew 22:37-40). God accepts us just as we are. And, if He accepts us—faults and all—then who are we to believe otherwise?

One of Satan's most effective ploys is to make us believe that we are small, insignificant, and worthless.

Susan Lenzkes

Give yourself a gift today:
be present with yourself. God is.
Enjoy your own personality. God does.

Barbara Johnson

I may have tasted peace, but to believe that the God of heaven and earth calls me beautiful—well, I think I could rest in that. If I truly knew that He was smitten with me, maybe I could take a deep breath, square my shoulders, and go out to face the world with confidence.

Angela Thomas

Yes, we need to acknowledge our weaknesses, to confess our sins. But if we want to be active, productive participants in the realm of God, we also need to recognize our gifts, to appreciate our strengths, to build on the abilities God has given us. We need to balance humility with confidence.

Penelope Stokes

Being loved by Him whose opinion matters most gives us the security to risk loving, too—even loving ourselves.

Gloria Gaither

As I have grown in faith and confidence, I have known more and more that my worth is based on the love of God.

Leslie Williams

Christian women are often blocked from maximizing their potential because they do not understand the power of the Holy Spirit within them. Many Christian women struggle with the I'm-not-good-enough-smart-enough-talented-enough syndrome. A leader of women understands that every daughter of the King has been uniquely designed and equipped for a purpose.

Susan Hunt

We will never be happy until we make God the source of our fulfillment and the answer to our longings.

Stormie Omartian

MORE FROM GOD'S WORD

For You have made him a little lower than the angels, and You have crowned him with glory and honor.

Psalm 8:5 NKJV

How happy are those whose way is blameless, who live according to the law of the Lord! Happy are those who keep His decrees and seek Him with all their heart.

Psalm 119:1-2 HCSB

Happy is the one whose help is the God of Jacob, whose hope is in the Lord his God.

Psalm 146:5 HCSB

If God is for us, who is against us?

Romans 8:31 HCSB

Finally, brethren, whatever things are true, whatever things are noble, whatever things are just, whatever things are pure, whatever things are lovely, whatever things are of good report, if there is any virtue and if there is anything praiseworthy—meditate on these things.

Philippians 4:8 NKJV

I say to myself, "The LORD is my inheritance;
therefore, I will hope in him!"

Lamentations 3:24 NLT

SHADES OF GRACE

Living by grace inspires a growing consciousness that I am what I am in the sight of Jesus and nothing more. It is His approval that counts.

Brennan Manning

A PRAYER FOR TODAY

Lord, I have so much to learn and so many ways to improve myself, but You love me just as I am. Thank You for Your love and for Your Son. And, help me to become the person that You want me to become. Amen

Praising God for His Abundance

I came that they may have life, and have it abundantly.

John 10:10 NASB

God's gifts are available to all, but they are not guaranteed; those gifts must be claimed by those who choose to follow Christ. As believers, we are free to accept God's gifts, or not; that choice, and the consequences that result from it, are ours and ours alone.

The 10th chapter of John tells us that Christ came to earth so that our lives might be filled with abundance. But what, exactly, did Jesus mean when He promised "life...more abundantly"? Was Jesus referring to material possessions or financial wealth? Hardly. When Jesus declared Himself the shepherd of mankind (John 10:7-9), He offered a different kind of abundance: a spiritual richness that extends beyond the temporal boundaries of this world.

If you are a thoughtful believer, you will open yourself to Christ's spiritual abundance by following

Him completely and without reservation. When you do, you will receive the love, the peace, and the joy that He has promised.

The fullness of life in Christ is available to all who seek it and claim it. Count yourself among that number. Seek first the salvation that is available through a personal relationship with Jesus, and then claim the abundance that can—and should—be yours.

Do you sincerely seek the riches that our Savior offers to those who give themselves to Him? Then follow Him—and receive the blessings that He has promised. When you establish an intimate, passionate relationship with Christ, you are then free to claim the love, the protection, and the spiritual abundance that the Shepherd offers His sheep.

Get ready for God to show you not only His pleasure, but His approval.

Joni Eareckson Tada

Yes, we were created for His holy pleasure, but we will ultimately—if not immediately—find much pleasure in His pleasure.

Beth Moore

More from God's Word

Live in me. Make your home in me just as I do in you. In the same way that a branch can't bear grapes by itself but only by being joined to the vine, you can't bear fruit unless you are joined with me. I am the Vine, you are the branches. When you're joined with me and I with you, the relation intimate and organic, the harvest is sure to be abundant.

John 15:4-5 MSG

Until now you have asked for nothing in My name. Ask and you will receive, that your joy may be complete.

John 16:24 HCSB

The master was full of praise. "Well done, my good and faithful servant. You have been faithful in handling this small amount, so now I will give you many more responsibilities. Let's celebrate together!"

Matthew 25:21 NLT

If you give, you will receive. Your gift will return to you in full measure, pressed down, shaken together to make room for more, and running over. Whatever measure you use in giving—large or small—it will be used to measure what is given back to you.

Luke 6:38 NLT

*Come to terms with God and be at peace;
in this way good will come to you.*

Job 22:21 HCSB

SHADES OF GRACE

Grace is an outrageous blessing bestowed freely
on a totally undeserving recipient.

Bill Hybels

A PRAYER FOR TODAY

*I praise You, Lord, for the abundant life given through Your
Son Jesus Christ. You have blessed me beyond measure.
Make me a faithful steward of the gifts You have given me
so that I may share Your abundance with all who cross my
path. Amen*

The Need for Silence

Be silent before the Lord and wait expectantly for Him.

Psalm 37:7 HCSB

The world seems to grow louder day by day, and our senses seem to be invaded at every turn. If we allow the distractions of a clamorous society to separate us from God's peace, we do ourselves a profound disservice. Our task, as believers, is to carve out moments of silence in a world filled with noise.

If we are to maintain righteous minds and compassionate hearts, we must take time each day for prayer and for meditation. We must make ourselves still in the presence of our Creator. We must quiet our minds and our hearts so that we might sense God's will and His love.

Has the hectic pace of life robbed you of God's peace? If so, it's time to reorder your priorities and your life. Nothing is more important than the time you spend with your Heavenly Father. So be still and claim the genuine peace that is found in the silent moments you spend with God.

If you, too, will learn to wait upon God, to get alone with Him, and remain silent so that you can hear His voice when He is ready to speak to you, what a difference it will make in your life!

Kay Arthur

I always begin my prayers in silence, for it is in the silence of the heart that God speaks.

Mother Teresa

Deepest communion with God is beyond words, on the other side of silence.

Madeleine L'Engle

The world is full of noise. Might we not set ourselves to learn silence, stillness, solitude?

Elisabeth Elliot

Be still, and in the quiet moments, listen to the voice of your Heavenly Father. His words can renew your spirit. No one knows you and your needs like He does.

Janet L. Weaver

Jesus taught us by example to get out of the rat race and recharge our batteries.

Barbara Johnson

My soul, wait silently for God alone,
For my expectation is from Him.

Psalm 62:5 NKJV

SHADES OF GRACE

Surely it has theological significance that un-earned gifts and unexpected pleasures bring the most joy. Grace billows up.

Philip Yancey

A PRAYER FOR TODAY

Dear Lord, in the quiet moments of this day, I will turn my thoughts and prayers to You. In silence I will sense Your presence, and I will seek Your will for my life, knowing that when I accept Your peace, I will be blessed today and throughout eternity. Amen

Making Time for God

Don't burn out; keep yourselves fueled and aflame. Be alert servants of the Master, cheerfully expectant. Don't quit in hard times; pray all the harder.

Romans 12:11-12 MSG

Has the busy pace of life robbed you of the peace that might otherwise be yours through Jesus Christ? If so, you are simply too busy for your own good. Through His Son Jesus, God offers you a peace that passes human understanding, but He won't force His peace upon you; in order to experience it, you must slow down long enough to sense His presence and His love.

Each waking moment holds the potential to think a creative thought or offer a heartfelt prayer. So even if you're a woman with too many demands and too few hours in which to meet them, don't panic. Instead, be comforted in the knowledge that when you sincerely seek to discover God's purpose for your life, He will respond in marvelous and surprising ways. Remember: this is the day that He has made and that He has filled it with countless opportunities to love, to serve, and to seek His guidance. Seize those opportunities today, and keep seizing them every day that you live.

We all long for that more sane lifestyle rather than being overwhelmed.

Patsy Clairmont

When a church member gets overactive and public worship is neglected, his or her relationship with God will be damaged.

Anne Ortlund

In our tense, uptight society where folks are rushing to make appointments they have already missed, a good laugh can be a refreshing as a cup of cold water in the desert.

Barbara Johnson

Life is not intended to be simply a round of work, no matter how interesting and important that work may be. A moment's pause to watch the glory of a sunrise or a sunset is soul satisfying, while a bird's song will set the steps to music all day long.

Laura Ingalls Wilder

MORE FROM GOD'S WORD

Careful planning puts you ahead in the long run; hurry and scurry puts you further behind.

Proverbs 21:5 MSG

You can't go wrong when you love others. When you add up everything in the law code, the sum total is love. But make sure that you don't get so absorbed and exhausted in taking care of all your day-by-day obligations that you lose track of the time and doze off, oblivious to God.

Romans 13:10-11 MSG

Jesus said, "You're tied down to the mundane; I'm in touch with what is beyond your horizons. You live in terms of what you see and touch. I'm living on other terms. I told you that you were missing God in all this. You're at a dead end. If you won't believe I am who I say I am, you're at the dead end of sins. You're missing God in your lives."

John 8:23-24 MSG

Let us fix our eyes on Jesus, the author and perfecter of our faith, who for the joy set before him endured the cross, scorning its shame, and sat down at the right hand of the throne of God.

Hebrews 12:2 NIV

97

It's obvious, isn't it? The place where your treasure is, is the place you will most want to be, and end up being.

Luke 12:34 MSG

SHADES OF GRACE

Yes, God's grace is always sufficient, and His arms are always open to give it. But, will our arms be open to receive it?

Beth Moore

A PRAYER FOR TODAY

Dear Lord, You are my rock, and I praise You for Your blessings. But sometimes, I am distracted by the busyness of the day or the demands of the moment. When I am worried or anxious, Father, turn my thoughts back to You. Help me to trust Your will, to follow Your commands, and to accept Your peace, today and forever. Amen

Trust His Perfect Plan

You will show me the path of life; in Your presence is fullness of joy; at Your right hand are pleasures forevermore.

Psalm 16:11 NKJV

God has a plan for your life. He understands that plan as thoroughly and completely as He knows you. And, if you seek God's will earnestly and prayerfully, He will make His plans known to you in His own time and in His own way.

If you sincerely seek to live in accordance with God's will for your life, you will live in accordance with His commandments. You will study God's Word, and you will be watchful for His signs.

Sometimes, God's plans seem unmistakably clear to you. But other times, He may lead you through the wilderness before He directs you to the Promised Land. So be patient and keep seeking His will for your life. When you do, you'll be amazed at the marvelous things that an all-powerful, all-knowing God can do.

God in Christ is the author and finisher of my faith. He knows exactly what needs to happen in my life for my faith to grow. He designs the perfect program for me.

Mary Morrison Suggs

Obedience to God is our job.
The results of that obedience are God's.

Elisabeth Elliot

When the dream of our heart is one that God has planted there, a strange happiness flows into us. At that moment, all of the spiritual resources of the universe are released to help us. Our praying is then at one with the will of God and becomes a channel for the Creator's purposes for us and our world.

Catherine Marshall

God has plans—not problems—for our lives. Before she died in the concentration camp in Ravensbruck, my sister Betsie said to me, "Corrie, your whole life has been a training for the work you are doing here in prison—and for the work you will do afterward."

Corrie ten Boom

I'm convinced that there is nothing that can happen to me in this life that is not precisely designed by a sovereign Lord to give me the opportunity to learn to know Him.

Elisabeth Elliot

God has His reasons. He has His purposes. Ours is an intentional God, brimming over with motive and mission. He never does things capriciously or decides with the flip of a coin.

Joni Eareckson Tada

God prepared a plan for your life alone—and neither man nor the devil can destroy that plan.

Kay Arthur

God has ordained that others may see the reality of His presence by the illumination our lives shed forth.

Beth Moore

The Lord never makes a mistake. One day, when we are in heaven, I'm sure we shall see the answers to all the whys. My, how often I have asked, "Why?" In heaven, we shall see God's side of the embroidery.

Corrie ten Boom

101

MORE FROM GOD'S WORD

"I say this because I know what I am planning for you,"
says the Lord. "I have good plans for you, not plans to hurt
you. I will give you hope and a good future."

Jeremiah 29:11 NCV

People may make plans in their minds, but the Lord decides
what they will do.

Proverbs 16:9 NCV

There is no wisdom, no insight, no plan that can succeed
against the Lord.

Proverbs 21:30 NIV

Unless the Lord builds a house, the work of the builders is
useless.

Psalm 127:1 NLT

The Lord says, "I will guide you along the best pathway for
your life. I will advise you and watch over you."

Psalm 32:8 NLT

The Lord is the strength of my life.

Psalm 27:1 KJV

*However, each one must live his life
in the situation the Lord assigned
when God called him.*

1 Corinthians 7:17 HCSB

SHADES OF GRACE

We're not only saved by grace, but the Bible says we're sustained by grace.

Bill Hybels

A PRAYER FOR TODAY

Lord, You have a plan for my life that is grander than I can imagine. Let Your purposes be my purposes. Let Your will be my will. When I am confused, give me clarity. When I am frightened, give me courage. Let me be Your faithful servant, always seeking Your guidance for my life. And, let me always be a shining beacon for Your Son today and every day that I live. Amen

Finding Comfort

Praise be to the God and Father of our Lord Jesus Christ. God is the Father who is full of mercy and all comfort. He comforts us every time we have trouble, so when others have trouble, we can comfort them with the same comfort God gives us.

2 Corinthians 1:3-4 NCV

As Christians, we can be assured of this fact: Whether we find ourselves on the pinnacle of the mountain or in the darkest depths of the valley, God is there.

If you have been touched by the transforming love of Jesus, then you have every reason to live courageously. After all, Christ has already won the ultimate battle—and He won it for you—on the cross at Calvary. Still, even if you are a dedicated Christian, you may find yourself discouraged by the inevitable disappointments and tragedies that occur in the lives of believers and non-believers alike.

The next time you find your courage tested to the limit, lean upon God's promises. Trust His Son.

Remember that God is always near and that He is your protector and your deliverer. When you are worried, anxious, or afraid, call upon Him and accept the touch of His comforting hand. Remember that God rules both mountaintops and valleys—with limitless wisdom and love—now and forever.

What a comfort to know that God is present
there in your life, available to meet
every situation with you,
that you are never left to face
any problem alone.

Vonette Bright

Put your hand into the hand of God. He gives the calmness and serenity of heart and soul.

Mrs. Charles E. Cowman

O Lord, thank You that Your side of the embroidery of our life is always perfect. That is such a comfort when our side is sometimes so mixed up.

Corrie ten Boom

When faced with adversity the Christian woman comforts herself with the knowledge that all of life's events are in the hands of God.

Vonette Bright

Don't be overwhelmed. Take it one day and one prayer at a time.

Stormie Omartian

Obedience invites Christ to show His incomparable strength in our mortal weakness.

Beth Moore

If God has you in the palm of His hand and your real life is secure in Him, then you can venture forth—into the places and relationships, the challenges, the very heart of the storm—and you will be safe there.

Paula Rinehart

MORE FROM GOD'S WORD

Carry each other's burdens, and in this way you will fulfill the law of Christ.

Galatians 6:2 NIV

Finally, all of you be of one mind, having compassion for one another; love as brothers, be tenderhearted, be courteous.

1 Peter 3:8 NKJV

So, as those who have been chosen of God, holy and beloved, put on a heart of compassion, kindness, humility, gentleness and patience.

Colossians 3:12 NASB

But he's already made it plain how to live, what to do, what God is looking for in men and women. It's quite simple: Do what is fair and just to your neighbor, be compassionate and loyal in your love, and don't take yourself too seriously—take God seriously.

Micah 6:8 MSG

Humble yourselves therefore under the mighty hand of God, so that He may exalt you in due time, casting all your care upon Him, because He cares about you.

1 Peter 5:6-7 HCSB

The Lord is my rock, my fortress and my savior;
my God is my rock in whom I find protection.
He is my shield, the strength of my salvation,
and my stronghold.

Psalm 18:2 NLT

SHADES OF GRACE

The grace of God runs downhill toward the ones who are emptied and vulnerable, toward the ones who admit that they struggle.

Angela Thomas

A PRAYER FOR TODAY

Today, Lord, let me count my blessings with thanksgiving in my heart. You have cared for me, Lord, and I will give You the glory and the praise. Let me accept Your blessings and Your gifts, and let me share them with others, just as You first shared them with me. Amen

Acceptance Today

One thing I do, forgetting those things which are behind and reaching forward to those things which are ahead, I press toward the goal for the prize of the upward call of God in Christ Jesus.

Philippians 3:13-14 NKJV

Manmade plans are fallible; God's plans are not. Yet whenever life takes an unexpected turn, we are tempted to fall into the spiritual traps of worry, self-pity, or bitterness. God intends that we do otherwise.

The old saying is familiar: "Forgive and forget." But when we have been hurt badly, forgiveness is often difficult and forgetting is downright impossible. Since we can't forget yesterday's troubles, we should learn from them. Yesterday has much to teach us about tomorrow. We may learn from the past, but we should never live in the past.

So if you're trying to forget the past, don't waste your time. Instead, try a different approach: learn to accept the past and live in the present. Then, you can focus your thoughts and your energies, not on the struggles of yesterday, but instead on the profound opportunities that God has placed before you today.

Surrender to the Lord is not a tremendous
sacrifice, not an agonizing performance.
It is the most sensible thing you can do.

Corrie ten Boom

He does not need to transplant us into a different field. He transforms the very things that were before our greatest hindrances, into the chief and most blessed means of our growth. No difficulties in your case can baffle Him. Put yourself absolutely into His hands, and let Him have His own way with you.

Elisabeth Elliot

It is always possible to do the will of God. In every place and time it is within our power to acquiesce in the will of God.

Elisabeth Elliot

I pray hard, work hard, and leave the rest to God.

Florence Griffith Joyner

Contentment has a way of quieting insatiable desires.

Mary Hunt

Mature people are not emotionally and spiritually devastated by every mistake they make. They are able to maintain some kind of balance in their lives.

Joyce Meyer

Ultimately things work out best for those who make the best of the way things work out.

Barbara Johnson

MORE FROM GOD'S WORD

A man's heart plans his way, but the Lord determines his steps.

Proverbs 16:9 HCSB

For everything created by God is good, and nothing should be rejected if it is received with thanksgiving.

1 Timothy 4:4 HCSB

Should we accept only good from God and not adversity?

Job 2:10 HCSB

He is the Lord. Let him do what he thinks is best.

1 Samuel 3:18 NCV

Sheathe your sword! Should I not drink the cup that the Father has given Me?

John 18:11 HCSB

Can you understand the secrets of God? His limits are higher than the heavens; you cannot reach them! They are deeper than the grave; you cannot understand them! His limits are longer than the earth and wider than the sea.

Job 11:7-9 NCV

Human plans, no matter how wise or well advised, cannot stand against the LORD.

Proverbs 21:30 NLT

SHADES OF GRACE

The grace of God means something like: Here is your life. You might never have been, but you are because the party wouldn't have been complete without you. Here is the world. Beautiful and terrible things will happen. Don't be afraid. I am with you. Nothing can ever separate us. It's for you I created the universe. I love you.

Frederick Buechner

A PRAYER FOR TODAY

Lord, when I am discouraged, give me hope. When I am impatient, give me peace. When I face circumstances that I cannot change, give me a spirit of acceptance. In all things great and small, let me trust in You, Dear Lord, knowing that You are the Giver of life and the Giver of all things good, today and forever. Amen

Listening to God

The one who is from God listens to God's words. This is why you don't listen, because you are not from God.

John 8:47 HCSB

Sometimes, God displays His wishes in ways that are undeniable. But on other occasions, the hand of God is much more subtle than that. Sometimes, God speaks to us in quiet tones, and when He does, we are well advised to listen . . . carefully.

Do you take time each day for an extended period of silence? And during those precious moments, do you sincerely open your heart to your Creator? If so, you are wise and you are blessed.

The world can be a noisy place, a place filled to the brim with distractions, interruptions, and frustrations. And if you're not careful, the struggles and stresses of everyday living can rob you of the peace that should rightfully be yours because of your personal relationship with Christ. So take time each day to quietly commune with your Savior. When you do, you will most certainly encounter the subtle hand of

God, and if you are wise, you will let His hand lead you along the path that He has chosen.

We need to stop focusing on our lacks and stop giving out excuses and start looking at and listening to Jesus.

Anne Graham Lotz

When I am constantly running there is no time for being. When there is no time for being there is no time for listening.

Madeleine L'Engle

The pathway of obedience can sometimes be difficult, but it always leads to a strengthening of our inner woman.

Vonette Bright

When we come to Jesus stripped of pretensions, with a needy spirit, ready to listen, He meets us at the point of need.

Catherine Marshall

We need to stop focusing on our lacks and stop giving out excuses and start looking at and listening to Jesus.

Anne Graham Lotz

MORE FROM GOD'S WORD

God has no use for the prayers of the people who won't listen to him.

Proverbs 28:9 MSG

Trust God from the bottom of your heart; don't try to figure out everything on your own. Listen for God's voice in everything you do, everywhere you go; he's the one who will keep you on track.

Proverbs 3:5-6 MSG

You must follow the Lord your God and fear Him. You must keep His commands and listen to His voice; you must worship Him and remain faithful to Him.

Deuteronomy 13:4 HCSB

Then if my people who are called by my name will humble themselves and pray and seek my face and turn from their wicked ways, I will hear from heaven and will forgive their sins and heal their land.

2 Chronicles 7:14 NLT

Listen in silence before me....

Isaiah 41:1 NLT

SHADES OF GRACE

God shares Himself generously and graciously.

Eugene Peterson

A PRAYER FOR TODAY

Dear Lord, I have so much to learn and You have so much to teach me. Give me the wisdom to be still and the discernment to hear Your voice, today and every day. Amen

He Gives Us Hope

Without wavering, let us hold tightly to the hope we say we have, for God can be trusted to keep his promise.

Hebrews 10:23 NLT

Despite God's promises, despite Christ's love, and despite our countless blessings, we frail human beings can still lose hope from time to time. When we do, we need the encouragement of Christian friends, the life-changing power of prayer, and the healing truth of God's Holy Word.

If you find yourself falling into the spiritual traps of worry and discouragement, seek the healing touch of Jesus and the encouraging words of fellow Christians. And remember the words of our Savior: "These things I have spoken unto you, that in me ye might have peace. In the world ye shall have tribulation: but be of good cheer; I have overcome the world" (John 16:33 KJV). This world can be a place of trials and tribulations, but as believers, we are secure. God has promised us peace, joy, and eternal life. And, of course, God keeps His promises today, tomorrow, and forever.

No other religion, no other philosophy promises new bodies, hearts, and minds. Only in the Gospel of Christ do hurting people find such incredible hope.

Joni Eareckson Tada

In those desperate times when we feel like we don't have an ounce of strength, He will gently pick up our heads so that our eyes can behold something— something that will keep His hope alive in us.

Kathy Troccoli

The choice for me is to either look at all things I have lost or the things I have. To live in fear or to live in hope…. Hope comes from knowing I have a sovereign, loving God who is in every event in my life.

Lisa Beamer (Her husband Todd was killed on flight 93, 9-11-01)

Hope is the desire and the ability to move forward.

Emilie Barnes

Love is the seed of all hope. It is the enticement to trust, to risk, to try, and to go on.

Gloria Gaither

I discovered that sorrow was not to be feared but rather endured with hope and expectancy that God would use it to visit and bless my life.

Jill Briscoe

Stop thinking wishfully and start living hopefully.

Emilie Barnes

Hope looks for the good in people, opens doors for people, discovers what can be done to help, lights a candle, does not yield to cynicism. Hope sets people free.

Barbara Johnson

Make the least of all that goes and the most of all that comes. Don't regret what is past. Cherish what you have. Look forward to all that is to come. And most important of all, rely moment by moment on Jesus Christ.

Gigi Graham Tchividjian

MORE FROM GOD'S WORD

For I know the thoughts that I think toward you, says the Lord, thoughts of peace and not of evil, to give you a future and a hope. Then you will call upon Me and go and pray to Me, and I will listen to you.

Jeremiah 29:11-12 NKJV

Hope deferred makes the heart sick.

Proverbs 13:12 NKJV

Sustain me as You promised, and I will live; do not let me be ashamed of my hope.

Psalm 119:116 HCSB

Be of good courage, and He shall strengthen your heart, all you who hope in the Lord.

Psalm 31:24 NKJV

But the Lord is faithful; he will make you strong and guard you from the evil one.

2 Thessalonians 3:3 NLT

I wait for the Lord;
I wait, and put my hope in His word.
Psalm 130:5 HCSB

SHADES OF GRACE

Abounding sin is the terror of the world, but abounding grace is the hope of mankind.

A. W. Tozer

A PRAYER FOR TODAY

Dear Lord, make me a woman of hope. If I become discouraged, let me turn to You. If I grow weary, let me seek strength in You. When I face disappointments, let me seek Your will and trust Your Word. In every aspect of my life, I will trust You, Father, so that my heart will be filled with faith, hope, and praise, this day and forever. Amen

Making Peace with the Past

Your old life is dead. Your new life, which is your real life—even though invisible to spectators—is with Christ in God. He is your life.

Colossians 3:3 MSG

The American theologian Reinhold Niebuhr composed a profoundly simple verse that came to be known as the Serenity Prayer: "God, grant me the serenity to accept the things I cannot change, the courage to change the things I can, and the wisdom to know the difference." Niebuhr's words are far easier to recite than they are to live by. Why? Because most of us want life to unfold in accordance with our own wishes and timetables. But sometimes God has other plans.

One of the things that fits nicely into the category of "things we cannot change" is the past. Yet even though we know that the past is unchangeable, many of us continue to invest energy worrying about the unfairness of yesterday (when we should, instead, be focusing on the opportunities of today and the promises of tomorrow). Author Hannah Whitall Smith observed, "How changed our lives would be if we could only fly through the days on wings of surrender and trust!" These words remind us that even when we cannot understand the past, we must trust God and accept His will.

So, if you've endured a difficult past, accept it and learn from it, but don't spend too much time here in the precious present fretting over memories of the unchangeable past. Instead, trust God's plan and look to the future. After all, the future is where everything that's going to happen to you from this moment on is going to take place.

Create in me a pure heart, O God,
and renew a steadfast spirit within me.
Psalm 51:10 NIV

Our yesterdays teach us how to savor our todays and tomorrows.

Patsy Clairmont

If you are God's child, you are no longer bound to your past or to what you were. You are a brand new creature in Christ Jesus.

Kay Arthur

No matter what, don't ever let yesterday use up too much of today.

Barbara Johnson

Whoever you are, whatever your condition or circumstance, whatever your past or problem, Jesus can restore you to wholeness.

Anne Graham Lotz

We set our eyes on the finish line, forgetting the past, and straining toward the mark of spiritual maturity and fruitfulness.

Vonette Bright

125

And He who sits on the throne said,
"Behold, I am making all things new."
Revelation 21:5 NASB

SHADES OF GRACE

The grace of God is the one thing we cannot do without in this life or in the life to come; it has no substitutes, artificial, temporary, or otherwise.

Bill Bright

A PRAYER FOR TODAY

Heavenly Father, free me from anger, resentment, and envy. When I am bitter, I cannot feel the peace that You intend for my life. Keep me mindful that forgiveness is Your commandment, and help me accept the past, treasure the present, and trust the future . . . to You. Amen

Trusting God's Will

Teach me to do Your will, for You are my God; Your Spirit is good. Lead me in the land of uprightness.

Psalm 143:10 NKJV

The Book of Judges tells the story of Deborah, the fearless woman who helped lead the army of Israel to victory over the Canaanites. Deborah was a judge and a prophetess, a woman called by God to lead her people. And when she answered God's call, she was rewarded with one of the great victories of Old Testament times.

Like Deborah, all of us are called to serve our Creator. And, like Deborah, we may sometimes find ourselves facing trials that can bring trembling to the very depths of our souls. As believers, we must seek God's will and follow it. When we do, we are rewarded with victories, some great and some small. When we entrust our lives to Him completely and without reservation, He gives us the strength to meet any challenge, the courage to face any trial, and the wisdom to live in His righteousness and in His peace.

The only safe place is in the center of God's will. It is not only the safest place. It is also the most rewarding and the most satisfying place to be.

Gigi Graham Tchividjian

The will of God is the most delicious and delightful thing in the universe.

Hannah Whitall Smith

Obedience is a foundational stepping stone on the path of God's Will.

Elizabeth George

I believe that in every time and place it is within our power to acquiesce in the will of God—and what peace it brings to do so!

Elisabeth Elliot

As you place yourself under the sovereign lordship of Jesus Christ, each mistake or failure can lead you right back to the throne.

Barbara Johnson

The center of power is not to be found in summit meetings or in peace conferences. It is not in Peking or Washington or the United Nations, but rather where a child of God prays in the power of the Spirit for God's will to be done in her life, in her home, and in the world around her.

Ruth Bell Graham

In the Garden of Gethsemane, Jesus went through agony of soul in His efforts to resist the temptation to do what He felt like doing rather than what He knew was God's will for Him.

Joyce Meyer

The choice for me is to either look at all things I have lost or the things I have. To live in fear or to live in hope. Hope comes from knowing I have a sovereign, loving God who is in every event in my life.

Lisa Beamer

Rejoicing is a matter of obedience to God—an obedience that will start you on the road to peace and contentment.

Kay Arthur

More from God's Word

He is the Lord. He will do what He thinks is good.

1 Samuel 3:18 HCSB

Teach me your ways, O LORD, that I may live according to your truth! Grant me purity of heart, that I may honor you.

Psalm 86:11 NLT

Commit your activities to the Lord and your plans will be achieved.

Proverbs 16:3 HCSB

And this world is fading away, along with everything it craves. But if you do the will of God, you will live forever.

1 John 2:17 NLT

Whoever does the will of God is My brother and sister and mother.

Mark 3:35 HCSB

The LORD is close to the brokenhearted and saves those who are crushed in spirit.

Psalm 34:18 NIV

*I wait quietly before God, for my salvation
comes from him. He alone is my rock
and my salvation, my fortress where
I will never be shaken.*

Psalm 62:1-2 NLT

SHADES OF GRACE

God is so gracious that He will even take us
when we use Him as our last resort.

C. S. Lewis

A PRAYER FOR TODAY

*Lord, let Your will be my will. When I am confused, give
me maturity and wisdom. When I am worried, give me
courage and strength. Let me be Your faithful servant,
Father, always seeking Your guidance and Your will for
my life. Amen*

DAY 27

His Grace Is Sufficient

My grace is sufficient for you, for My strength is made perfect in weakness.

2 Corinthians 12:9 NKJV

Of this you can be sure: the loving heart of God is sufficient to meet your needs. Whatever dangers you may face, whatever heartbreaks you must endure, God is with you, and He stands ready to comfort you and to heal you.

The Psalmist writes, "Weeping may endure for a night, but joy comes in the morning" (Psalm 30:5 NKJV). But when we are suffering, the morning may seem very far away. It is not. God promises that He is "near to those who have a broken heart" (Psalm 34:18 NKJV. In times of intense sadness, we must turn to Him, and we must encourage our friends and family members to do likewise.

If you are experiencing the intense pain of a recent loss, or if you are still mourning a loss from long ago, perhaps you are now ready to begin the next stage of your journey with God. If so, be mindful of this fact:

the loving heart of God is sufficient to meet any challenge, including yours. Trust the sufficient heart of God.

Snuggle in God's arms. When you are hurting, when you feel lonely or left out, let Him cradle you, comfort you, reassure you of His all-sufficient power and love.

Kay Arthur

Like Paul, we may bear thorns so that we can discover God's perfect sufficiency.

Beth Moore

The last and greatest lesson that the soul has to learn is the fact that God, and God alone, is enough for all its needs. This is the lesson that all His dealings with us are meant to teach; and this is the crowning discovery of our whole Christian life. God is enough!

Hannah Whitall Smith

Joy is a by-product not of happy circumstances, education or talent, but of a healthy relationship with God and a determination to love Him no matter what.

Barbara Johnson

Now the God of all grace, who called you
to His eternal glory in Christ Jesus,
will personally restore, establish,
strengthen, and support you.

1 Peter 5:10 HCSB

SHADES OF GRACE

The most amazing thing about grace to the suffering heart and soul is its utter sufficiency.

Bill Bright

A PRAYER FOR TODAY

Dear Lord, You are sufficient for my needs, and I praise
You. I will turn to You when I am fearful or worried. You
are my loving Heavenly Father, sufficient in all things and
I will always trust You. Amen

Beyond Worry

Worry is a heavy load . . . .

Proverbs 12:25 NCV

"Worry does not empty tomorrow of its sorrow; it empties today of its strength." So writes Corrie ten Boom, who survived a Nazi concentration camp during World War II. And while our own situations cannot be compared to Corrie's, we still worry about countless matters both great and small. Even though we are Christians who have been given the assurance of salvation—even though we are Christians who have received the promise of God's love and protection—we find ourselves fretting over the countless details of everyday life. Jesus understood our concerns when He spoke the reassuring words found in Matthew 6: "Therefore I tell you, do not worry about your life . . ."

As you consider the promises of Jesus, remember that God still sits in His heaven and you are His beloved child. Then, perhaps, you will worry a little less and trust God a little more, and that's as it should be because God is trustworthy . . . and you are protected.

Never yield to gloomy anticipation. Place your hope and confidence in God. He has no record of failure.

Mrs. Charles E. Cowman

Worries carry responsibilities that belong to God, not to you. Worry does not enable us to escape evil; it makes us unfit to cope with it when it comes.

Corrie ten Boom

Worry is the senseless process of cluttering up tomorrow's opportunities with leftover problems from today.

Barbara Johnson

Worship and worry cannot live in the same heart; they are mutually exclusive.

Ruth Bell Graham

We are meddling with God's business when we let all manner of imaginings loose, predicting disaster, contemplating possibilities instead of following, one day at a time, God's plain and simple pathway.

Elisabeth Elliot

Remember always that there are two things which are more utterly incompatible even than oil and water, and these two are trust and worry.

Hannah Whitall Smith

What is courage? It is the ability to be strong in trust, in conviction, in obedience. To be courageous is to step out in faith—to trust and obey, no matter what.

Kay Arthur

Because God is my sovereign Lord, I was not worried. He manages perfectly, day and night, year in and year out, the movements of the stars, the wheeling of the planets, the staggering coordination of events that goes on at the molecular level in order to hold things together. There is no doubt that He can manage the timing of my days and weeks.

Elisabeth Elliot

I do beg of you to recognize the extreme simplicity of faith; it is nothing more nor less than just believing God when He says He either has done something for us, or will do it; and then trusting Him to do it. It is so simple that it is hard to explain.

Hannah Whitall Smith

MORE FROM GOD'S WORD

Don't worry about anything, but in everything, through prayer and petition with thanksgiving, let your requests be made known to God.

Philippians 4:6 HCSB

Don't worry about your life, what you will eat or what you will drink; or about your body, what you will wear. Isn't life more than food and the body more than clothing?

Matthew 6:25 HCSB

I will be with you when you pass through the waters . . . when you walk through the fire . . . the flame will not burn you. For I the Lord your God, the Holy One of Israel, and your Savior.

Isaiah 43:2-3 HCSB

Your heart must not be troubled. Believe in God; believe also in Me.

John 14:1 HCSB

Trust in him at all times, O people; pour out your hearts to him, for God is our refuge.

Psalm 62:8 NIV

Cast your burden on the Lord,
and He will support you;
He will never allow the righteous to be shaken.

Psalm 55:22 HCSB

SHADES OF GRACE

God's grace and power seem to reach their peak
when we are at our weakest point.

Anne Graham Lotz

A PRAYER FOR TODAY

Lord, You sent Your Son to live as a man on this earth,
and You know what it means to be completely human.
You understand my worries and my fears, Lord, and You
forgive me when I am weak. When my faith begins to
wane, help me, Lord, to trust You more. Then, with Your
Holy Word on my lips and with the love of Your Son in my
heart, let me live courageously, faithfully, prayerfully, and
thankfully today and every day. Amen

The Cornerstone

The Lord is the strength of my life.

Psalm 27:1 KJV

Have you made God the cornerstone of your life, or is He relegated to a few hours on Sunday morning? Have you genuinely allowed God to reign over every corner of your heart, or have you attempted to place Him in a spiritual compartment? The answer to these questions will determine the direction of your day and your life.

God loves you. In times of trouble, He will comfort you; in times of sorrow, He will dry your tears. When you are weak or sorrowful, God is as near as your next breath. He stands at the door of your heart and waits. Welcome Him in and allow Him to rule. And then, accept the peace, and the strength, and the protection, and the abundance that only God can give.

You are mighty, Lord, you are mighty. Nothing compares to you in power. No one can equal the strength of your hand.

Mary Morrison Suggs

Measure the size of the obstacles against the size of God.

Beth Moore

So rejoice! You are giving Him what He asks you to give Him—the chance to show you what He can do.

Amy Carmichael

He goes before us, follows behind us, and hems us safe inside the realm of His protection.

Beth Moore

God walks with us. He scoops us up in His arms or simply sits with us in silent strength until we cannot avoid the awesome recognition that yes, even now, He is here.

Gloria Gaither

141

MORE FROM GOD'S WORD

But the Lord is faithful; he will make you strong and guard you from the evil one.

2 Thessalonians 3:3 NLT

You are the God who works wonders; You revealed Your strength among the peoples.

Psalm 77:14 HCSB

Come to me, all you who are weary and burdened, and I will give you rest. Take my yoke upon you and learn from me, for I am gentle and humble in heart, and you will find rest for your souls. For my yoke is easy and my burden is light.

Matthew 11:28-30 NIV

Fear not, for I am with you; be not dismayed, for I am your God. I will strengthen you, yes, I will help you, I will uphold you with My righteous right hand.

Isaiah 41:10 NKJV

I can do all things through Christ which strengtheneth me.

Philippians 4:13 KJV

God will never lead you where
His strength cannot keep you.

Barbara Johnson

SHADES OF GRACE

The grace of God is sufficient for all our needs,
for every problem, and for every difficulty, for
every broken heart, and for every human sorrow.

Peter Marshall

A PRAYER FOR TODAY

*Lord, You have promised never to leave me or forsake me.
You are always with me, protecting me and encouraging
me. Whatever this day may bring, I thank You for Your
love and for Your strength. Let me lean upon You, Father,
this day and forever. Amen*

He Forgives Us

Your beliefs about these things should be kept secret between you and God. People are happy if they can do what they think is right without feeling guilty.

Romans 14:22 NCV

All of us have sinned. Sometimes our sins result from our own stubborn rebellion against God's commandments. And sometimes, we are swept up in events that are beyond our abilities to control. Under either set of circumstances, we may experience intense feelings of guilt. But God has an answer for the guilt that we feel. That answer, of course, is His forgiveness. When we confess our wrongdoings and repent from them, we are forgiven by the One who created us.

Are you troubled by feelings of guilt or regret? If so, you must repent from your misdeeds, and ask your Heavenly Father for His forgiveness. When you do so, He will forgive you completely and without reservation. Then, you must forgive yourself just as God has forgiven you: thoroughly and unconditionally.

If God has forgiven you, why can't you forgive yourself?

Marie T. Freeman

If choosing to spend time alone with God is a real struggle—a heavy-handed demand that only adds more guilt and stress to your already overblown schedule—it's time to change the way you approach His presence.

Doris Greig

God sees everything we've ever done
and He's willing to forgive.
But we must confess to Him.

Ruth Bell Graham

Even in long-term grief there is a way to bring closure and to rise above the rage, the guilt, the pain. In Christ this is possible.

Barbara Johnson

One of Satan's most effective ploys is to make us believe that we are small, insignificant, and worthless.

Susan Lenzkes

Only God in Christ has the power to forgive sin. But you and I must confess it to Him personally, specifically, and honestly if we want to receive forgiveness.

Anne Graham Lotz

Stop blaming yourself and feeling guilty, unworthy, and unloved. Instead begin to say, "If God is for me, who can be against me? God loves me, and I love myself. Praise the Lord, I am free in Jesus' name, amen!"

Joyce Meyer

When I prayerfully remember my shortcomings, I'm not informing the Lord of anything He doesn't already know. But when I enumerate my failings, I take responsibility before Him, and He then releases me from dirty shame, grimy guilt, and scummy sin.

Patsy Clairmont

Full and true repentance is literally an about-face. It means turning completely around, away from sin, and turning toward God.

Shirley Dobson

MORE FROM GOD'S WORD

Be diligent to present yourself approved to God, a worker who doesn't need to be ashamed, correctly teaching the word of truth.

2 Timothy 2:15 HCSB

But God, who is abundant in mercy, because of His great love that He had for us, made us alive with the Messiah even though we were dead in trespasses. By grace you are saved!

Ephesians 2:4-5 HCSB

All the prophets testify about Him that through His name everyone who believes in Him will receive forgiveness of sins.

Acts 10:43 HCSB

There is therefore now no condemnation to those who are in Christ Jesus, who do not walk according to the flesh, but according to the Spirit.

Romans 8:1 NKJV

147

The one who conceals his sins will not prosper,
but whoever confesses and renounces
them will find mercy.

Proverbs 28:13 HCSB

SHADES OF GRACE

Grace is the good pleasure of God that inclines
Him to bestow benefits upon the undeserving.

A. W. Tozer

A PRAYER FOR TODAY

Dear Lord, thank You for the guilt that I feel when I
disobey You. Help me confess my wrongdoings, help me
accept Your forgiveness, and help me renew my passion to
serve You. Amen

The Power of Purpose

The lines of purpose in your lives never grow slack, tightly tied as they are to your future in heaven, kept taut by hope.

Colossians 1:5 MSG

"What on earth does God intend for me to do with my life?" It's an easy question to ask but, for many of us, a difficult question to answer. Why? Because God's purposes aren't always clear to us. Sometimes we wander aimlessly in a wilderness of our own making. And sometimes, we struggle mightily against God in an unsuccessful attempt to find success and happiness through our own means, not His.

Sometimes, God's intentions will be clear to you; other times, God's plan will seem uncertain at best. But even on those difficult days when you are unsure which way to turn, you must never lose sight of these overriding facts: God created you for a reason; He has important work for you to do; and He's waiting patiently for you to do it.

And the next step is up to you.

Only God's chosen task for you will ultimately satisfy. Do not wait until it is too late to realize the privilege of serving Him in His chosen position for you.

Beth Moore

His life is our light—our purpose and meaning and reason for living.

Anne Graham Lotz

In the very place where God has put us, whatever its limitations, whatever kind of work it may be, we may indeed serve the Lord Christ.

Elisabeth Elliot

How do I love God? By doing beautifully the work I have been given to do, by doing simply that which God entrusted to me, in whatever form it may take.

Mother Teresa

Yesterday is just experience but tomorrow is glistening with purpose—and today is the channel leading from one to the other.

Barbara Johnson

If you want to discover your spiritual gifts, start obeying God. As you serve Him, you will find that He has given you the gifts that are necessary to follow through in obedience.

Anne Graham Lotz

Obey God one step at a time, then the next step will come into view.

Catherine Marshall

How much of our lives are, well, so daily. How often our hours are filled with the mundane, seemingly unimportant things that have to be done, whether at home or work. These very "daily" tasks could become a celebration of praise. "It is through consecration," someone has said, "that drudgery is made divine."

Gigi Graham Tchividjian

Christian work is any kind of work, from cleaning a sewer to preaching a sermon, that is done by a Christian and offered to God.

Elisabeth Elliot

151

More from God's Word

For it is God who is working among you both the willing and the working for His good purpose.

Philippians 2:13 HCSB

We know that all things work together for the good of those who love God: those who are called according to His purpose.

Romans 8:28 HCSB

I will instruct you and show you the way to go; with My eye on you, I will give counsel.

Psalm 32:8 HCSB

You reveal the path of life to me; in Your presence is abundant joy; in Your right hand are eternal pleasures.

Psalm 16:11 HCSB

Then Jesus spoke to them again: "I am the light of the world. Anyone who follows Me will never walk in the darkness, but will have the light of life."

John 8:12 HCSB

*Commit your activities to the Lord and
your plans will be achieved.*

Proverbs 16:3 HCSB

SHADES OF GRACE

God's grand strategy, birthed in His grace toward us in Christ, and nurtured through the obedience of disciplined faith, is to release us into the redeemed life of our heart, knowing it will lead us back to Him even as the North Star guides a ship across the vast unknown surface of the ocean.

John Eldredge

A PRAYER FOR TODAY

Dear Lord, You are the Creator of the universe, and I know that Your plan for my life is grander than I can imagine. Let Your purposes be my purposes, and let me trust in the assurance of Your promises. Amen

153

The Power of Obedience

Follow the whole instruction the Lord your God has commanded you, so that you may live, prosper, and have a long life in the land you will possess.

Deuteronomy 5:33 HCSB

How can we demonstrate our love for God? By accepting His Son as our personal Savior and by placing Christ squarely at the center of our lives and our hearts. Jesus said that if we are to love Him, we must obey His commandments (John 14:15). Thus, our obedience to the Master is an expression of our love for Him.

In Ephesians 2:10 we read, "For we are His workmanship, created in Christ Jesus for good works." (NKJV). These words are instructive: We are not saved by good works, but for good works. Good works are not the root, but rather the fruit of our salvation.

Today, let the fruits of your stewardship be a clear demonstration of your love for Christ. When you do, your good heart will bring forth many good things for yourself and for God. Christ has given you spiritual abundance and eternal life. You, in turn, owe Him good treasure from a single obedient heart . . . yours.

Lord, as in heaven Your will is punctually performed, so may it be done on earth by all creatures, particularly in me and by me.

St. Elizabeth of Hungary

I know the power obedience has for making things easy which seem impossible.

St. Teresa of Avila

The pathway of obedience can sometimes be difficult, but it always leads to a strengthening of our inner woman.

Vonette Bright

Rejoicing is a matter of obedience to God—an obedience that will start you on the road to peace and contentment.

Kay Arthur

God is not hard to please. He does not expect us to be absolutely perfect. He just expects us to keep moving toward Him and believing in Him, letting Him work with us to bring us into conformity to His will and ways.

Joyce Meyer

Obedience goes before our hearts and carries them where they would not normally go.

Paula Rinehart

I pray women will choose the only way to true liberation by placing their faith in Jesus Christ as their own personal Savior, surrendering to Him as Lord, and serving Him as King.

Anne Graham Lotz

A wholehearted love for God looks to Him through His Word and prayer, always watching and waiting, ever ready to do all that He says, prepared to act on His expressed desires.

Elizabeth George

MORE FROM GOD'S WORD

I have sought You with all my heart; don't let me wander from Your commands.

Psalm 119:10 HCSB

Therefore, everyone who hears these words of Mine and acts on them will be like a sensible man who built his house on the rock. The rain fell, the rivers rose, and the winds blew and pounded that house. Yet it didn't collapse, because its foundation was on the rock.

Matthew 7:24–25 HCSB

Just then someone came up and asked Him, "Teacher, what good must I do to have eternal life?" "Why do you ask Me about what is good?" He said to him. "There is only One who is good. If you want to enter into life, keep the commandments."

Matthew 19:16-17 HCSB

Jesus answered, "If anyone loves Me, he will keep My word. My Father will love him, and We will come to him and make Our home with him."

John 14:23 HCSB

157

*The fear of the Lord is the beginning
of wisdom; all who follow
His instructions have good insight.*

Psalm 111:10 HCSB

SHADES OF GRACE

The step into the situation where faith is possible is not an offer which we can make to Jesus, but always His gracious offer to us. His initiative, our obedience.

Dietrich Bonhoeffer

A PRAYER FOR TODAY

Dear Lord, when I obey Your commandments, and when I trust the promises of Your Son, I experience love, peace, and abundance. Direct my path far from the temptations and distractions of this world. And, let me discover Your will and follow it, Dear Lord, this day and always. Amen

The Power of Optimism

Make me to hear joy and gladness.

Psalm 51:8 KJV

Are you an optimistic, hopeful, enthusiastic Christian? You should be. After all, as a believer, you have every reason to be optimistic about life here on earth and life eternal. As C. H. Spurgeon observed, "Our hope in Christ for the future is the mainstream of our joy." But sometimes, you may find yourself pulled down by the inevitable demands and worries of life-here-on-earth. If you find yourself discouraged, exhausted, or both, then it's time to take your concerns to God. When you do, He will lift your spirits and renew your strength.

Today, make this promise to yourself and keep it: vow to be a hope-filled Christian. Think optimistically about your life, your profession, your family, and your future. Trust your hopes, not your fears. Take time to celebrate God's glorious creation. Then, when you've filled your heart with hope and gladness, share your optimism with others.

We may run, walk, stumble, drive, or fly, but let us never lose sight of the reason for the journey, or miss a chance to see a rainbow on the way.

Gloria Gaither

Make the least of all that goes and the most of all that comes. Don't regret what is past. Cherish what you have. Look forward to all that is to come. And most important of all, rely moment by moment on Jesus Christ.

Gigi Graham Tchividjian

Knowing God's sovereignty and
unconditional love imparts
a beauty to life…and to you.

Kay Arthur

If you can't tell whether your glass is half-empty or half-full, you don't need another glass; what you need is better eyesight . . . and a more thankful heart.

Marie T. Freeman

Developing a positive attitude means working continually to find what is uplifting and encouraging.

Barbara Johnson

The Christian lifestyle is not one of legalistic do's and don'ts, but one that is positive, attractive, and joyful.

Vonette Bright

It never hurts your eyesight to look on the bright side of things.

Barbara Johnson

God specializes in things fresh and firsthand. His plans for you this year may outshine those of the past. He's prepared to fill your days with reasons to give Him praise.

Joni Eareckson Tada

Every day we live is a priceless gift of God, loaded with possibilities to learn something new, to gain fresh insights.

Dale Evans Rogers

161

Be of good courage,
and he shall strengthen your heart,
all ye that hope in the LORD.

Psalm 31:24 KJV

SHADES OF GRACE

Faith is a living, daring confidence in God's grace, so sure and certain that a man would stake his life on it a thousand times.

Martin Luther

A PRAYER FOR TODAY

Thank You, Lord, for Your infinite love. Make me an optimistic Christian, Father, as I place my hope and my trust in You. Amen

Worship Him

*For it is written, "You shall worship the Lord your God,
and Him only you shall serve."*

Matthew 4:10 NKJV

All of mankind is engaged in the practice of
worship. Some choose to worship God and,
as a result, reap the joy that He intends for
His children. Others distance themselves from God
by worshiping such things as earthly possessions or
personal gratification . . . and when they do so, they
suffer.

Today, as one way of worshipping God, make
every aspect of your life a cause for celebration and
praise. Praise God for the blessings and opportunities that He has given you, and live according to the
beautiful words found in the 5th chapter of 1 Thessalonians: "Rejoice evermore. Pray without ceasing. In
every thing give thanks: for this is the will of God in
Christ Jesus concerning you" (vv. 16-18 KJV).

God deserves your worship, your prayers, your
praise, and your thanks. And you deserve the joy that

is yours when you worship Him with your prayers, with your deeds, and with your life.

Worship always empowers the worshiper with a greater revelation of the object of her desire.

Lisa Bevere

It's our privilege to not only raise our hands in worship but also to combine the visible with the invisible in a rising stream of praise and adoration sent directly to our Father.

Shirley Dobson

God has promised to give you all of eternity. The least you can do is give Him one day a week in return.

Marie T. Freeman

God asks that we worship Him with our concentrated minds as well as with our wills and emotions. A divided and scattered mind is not effective.

Catherine Marshall

To worship Him in truth means to worship Him honestly, without hypocrisy, standing open and transparent before Him.

Anne Graham Lotz

Worship is God-centered, aware of one another only in that deep, joyous awareness of being caught up together in God.

Anne Ortlund

Make God's will the focus of your life day by day. If you seek to please Him and Him alone, you'll find yourself satisfied with life.

Kay Arthur

Spiritual worship comes from
our very core and is fueled by an awesome
reverence and desire for God.

Beth Moore

Our forgiveness of others becomes an act of worship that we would not enter into except for Who He is and for the overwhelming debt of love we owe Him.

Anne Graham Lotz

MORE FROM GOD'S WORD

I rejoiced with those who said to me, "Let us go to the house of the Lord."

Psalm 122:1 HCSB

But an hour is coming, and is now here, when the true worshipers will worship the Father in spirit and truth. Yes, the Father wants such people to worship Him. God is Spirit, and those who worship Him must worship in spirit and truth."

John 4:23-24 HCSB

For where two or three are gathered together in My name, I am there among them.

Matthew 18:20 HCSB

So that at the name of Jesus every knee should bow— of those who are in heaven and on earth and under the earth—and every tongue should confess that Jesus Christ is Lord, to the glory of God the Father.

Philippians 2:10-11 HCSB

All the earth will worship You and sing praise to You. They will sing praise to Your name.

Psalm 66:4 HCSB

The Lord values those who fear Him,
those who put their hope in His faithful love.

Psalm 147:11 HCSB

SHADES OF GRACE

No one is beyond His grace. No situation, anywhere on earth, is too hard for God.

Jim Cymbala

A PRAYER FOR TODAY

When I worship You, Lord, You direct my path and You cleanse my heart. Let today and every day be a time of worship and praise. Let me worship You in everything that I think and do. Thank You, Lord, for the priceless gift of Your Son Jesus. Let me be worthy of that gift, and let me give You the praise and the glory forever. Amen

Ask Him

Keep asking, and it will be given to you. Keep searching, and you will find. Keep knocking, and the door will be opened to you. For everyone who asks receives, and the one who searches finds, and to the one who knocks, the door will be opened.

Matthew 7:7-8 HCSB

Are you a woman who confidently asks God to move mountains, or do you timidly ask Him to push around a few molehills? God is perfectly capable of moving either molehills or mountains, so it's up to you to decide whether you want His help on big projects or tiny ones.

How often do you ask for God's help? Occasionally? Intermittently? Whenever you experience a crisis? Hopefully not. Hopefully, you have developed the habit of asking for God's assistance early and often. And hopefully, you have learned to seek His guidance in every aspect of your life.

God has promised that when you ask for His help, He will not withhold it. So ask. Ask Him to meet the needs of your day. Ask Him for wisdom. Ask Him to lead you, to protect you, and to correct you. And don't hesitate to ask Him to do big things in your own life and in the lives of your loved ones.

God stands at the door and waits. When you knock on His door, He answers. Your task, of course, is to seek His guidance prayerfully, confidently, and often.

We get into trouble when we think we know what to do and we stop asking God if we're doing it.

Stormie Omartian

Often I have made a request of God with earnest pleadings even backed up with Scripture, only to have Him say "No" because He had something better in store.

Ruth Bell Graham

By asking in Jesus' name, we're making a request not only in His authority, but also for His interests and His benefit.

Shirley Dobson

God uses our most stumbling, faltering faith-steps as the open door to His doing for us "more than we ask or think."

Catherine Marshall

When you ask God to do something, don't ask timidly; put your whole heart into it.

Marie T. Freeman

Cultivating a heart of prayer is a sure way to experience God's presence.

Elizabeth George

Real power in prayer flows only when a man's spirit touches God's spirit.

Catherine Marshall

When will we realize that we're not troubling God with our questions and concerns? His heart is open to hear us—His touch nearer than our next thought—as if no one in the world existed but us. Our very personal God wants to hear from us personally.

Gigi Graham Tchividjian

MORE FROM GOD'S WORD

So I say to you, keep asking, and it will be given to you. Keep searching, and you will find. Keep knocking, and the door will be opened to you.

Luke 11:9 HCSB

And in that day you will ask Me nothing. Most assuredly, I say to you, whatever you ask the Father in My name He will give you. Until now you have asked nothing in My name. Ask, and you will receive, that your joy may be full.

John 16:23-24 NKJV

Don't worry about anything, but in everything, through prayer and petition with thanksgiving, let your requests be made known to God.

Philippians 4:6 HCSB

For I know the thoughts that I think toward you, says the Lord, thoughts of peace and not of evil, to give you a future and a hope. Then you will call upon Me and go and pray to Me, and I will listen to you.

Jeremiah 29:11-12 NKJV

When a believing person prays,
great things happen.

James 5:16 NCV

SHADES OF GRACE

If we only believe and ask, a full measure of God's grace is available to any of us.

Charles Swindoll

A PRAYER FOR TODAY

Lord, when I have questions or fears, I will turn to You.
When I am weak, I will seek Your strength. When I am
discouraged, Father, I will be mindful of Your love and
Your grace. I will ask You for the things I need, Father, and
I will trust Your answers, today and forever. Amen

God's Calling

I, therefore, the prisoner in the Lord, urge you to walk worthy of the calling you have received.

Ephesians 4:1 HCSB

It is terribly important that you heed God's calling by discovering and developing your talents and your spiritual gifts. If you seek to make a difference—and if you seek to bear eternal fruit—you must discover your gifts and begin using them for the glory of God.

Every believer has at least one gift. In John 15:16, Jesus says, "You did not choose Me, but I chose you and appointed you that you should go and bear fruit, and that your fruit should remain, that whatever you ask the Father in My name He may give you." Have you found your special calling? If not, keep searching and keep praying until you find it. God has important work for you to do, and the time to begin that work is now.

Our Lord does not care so much for the importance of our works as for the love with which they are done.

St. Teresa of Avila

If God has called you, do not spend time looking over your shoulder to see who is following you.

Corrie ten Boom

If God's Word, your circumstances, and the counsel of others line up, and if you sense His provision, I'd say go for it.

Luci Swindoll

Most women have a sense of their spiritual side, even those who have no professed religion or organized affiliation with a belief system. They have a recognition that there is a way of life that works and that it's wrapped up in the spiritual.

Stormie Omartian

God calls us to seek Him daily in order to serve Him daily.

Sheila Cragg

God never calls without enabling us. In other words, if He calls you to do something, He makes it possible for you to do it.

Luci Swindoll

From the very moment one feels called to act is born the strength to bear whatever horror one will feel or see. In some inexplicable way, terror loses its overwhelming power when it becomes a task that must be faced.

Emmi Bonhoeffer

I may have tasted peace, but to believe that the God of heaven and earth calls me beautiful—well, I think I could rest in that. If I truly knew that He was smitten with me, maybe I could take a deep breath, square my shoulders, and go out to face the world with confidence.

Angela Thomas

Our progress in holiness depends on God and ourselves—on God's grace and on our will to be holy.

Mother Teresa

MORE FROM GOD'S WORD

But as God has distributed to each one, as the Lord has called each one, so let him walk.

1 Corinthians 7:17 NKJV

One thing I do, forgetting those things which are behind and reaching forward to those things which are ahead, I press toward the goal for the prize of the upward call of God in Christ Jesus.

Philippians 3:13-14 NKJV

So the last shall be first, and the first last: for many be called, but few chosen.

Matthew 20:16 KJV

For many are called, but few are chosen.

Matthew 22:14 KJV

We know that all things work together for the good of those who love God: those who are called according to His purpose.

Romans 8:28 HCSB

Teach me Your way, O Lord;
I will walk in Your truth.

Psalm 86:11 NKJV

SHADES OF GRACE

The Christian life is motivated, not by a list of do's and don'ts, but by the gracious outpouring of God's love and blessing.

Anne Graham Lotz

A PRAYER FOR TODAY

Heavenly Father, You have called me, and I acknowledge that calling. In these quiet moments before this busy day unfolds, I come to You. I will study Your Word and seek Your guidance. Give me the wisdom to know Your will for my life and the courage to follow wherever You may lead me, today and forever. Amen

Trusting God's Wisdom

Happy is the person who finds wisdom and gains understanding.

Proverbs 3:13 NLT

Sometimes, amid the concerns of everyday life, we lose perspective. Life seems out of balance as we confront an array of demands that sap our strength and cloud our thoughts. What's needed is a renewed faith, a fresh perspective, and God's wisdom.

Here in the 21st century, commentary is commonplace and information is everywhere. But the ultimate source of wisdom, the kind of timeless wisdom that God willingly shares with His children, is still available from a single unique source: the Holy Bible.

The wisdom of the world changes with the ever-shifting sands of public opinion. God's wisdom does not. His wisdom is eternal. It never changes. And it most certainly is the wisdom that you must use to plan your day, your life, and your eternal destiny.

This is my song through endless ages: Jesus led me all the way.

Fanny Crosby

He teaches us, not just to let us see ourselves correctly, but to help us see Him correctly.

Kathy Troccoli

If we neglect the Bible, we cannot expect to benefit from the wisdom and direction that result from knowing God's Word.

Vonette Bright

Knowledge can be found in books or in school. Wisdom, on the other hand, starts with God . . . and ends there.

Marie T. Freeman

If my life is surrendered to God, all is well. Let me not grab it back, as though it were in peril in His hand but would be safer in mine!

Elisabeth Elliot

You cannot grow spiritually until you have the assurance that Christ is in your life.

Vonette Bright

179

More from God's Word

The fear of the Lord is the beginning of wisdom; a good understanding have all those who do His commandments. His praise endures forever.

Psalm 111:10 NKJV

So teach us to number our days, that we may gain a heart of wisdom.

Psalm 90:12 NKJV

Teach me, O Lord, the way of Your statutes, and I shall keep it to the end.

Psalm 119:33 NKJV

A wise man will hear and increase learning, and a man of understanding will attain wise counsel.

Proverbs 1:5 NKJV

Acquire wisdom—how much better it is than gold! And acquire understanding—it is preferable to silver.

Proverbs 16:16 HCSB

One of the marks of Spiritual maturity
is a consistent, Spirit-controlled life.

Vonette Bright

SHADES OF GRACE

We will never cease to need our Father—His
wisdom, direction, help, and support. We will
never outgrow Him. We will always need His
grace.

Kay Arthur

A PRAYER FOR TODAY

*Dear Lord, when I trust in the wisdom of the world, I
am often led astray, but when I trust in Your wisdom, I
build my life upon a firm foundation. Today and every
day I will trust Your Word and follow it, knowing that the
ultimate wisdom is Your wisdom and the ultimate truth is
Your truth. Amen*

Beyond the Frustrations

When you are angry, do not sin, and be sure to stop being angry before the end of the day. Do not give the devil a way to defeat you.

Ephesians 4:26-27 NCV

Sometimes, anger is appropriate. Even Jesus became angry when confronted with the moneychangers in the temple. On occasion, you, like Jesus, will confront evil, and when you do, you may respond as He did: vigorously and without reservation. But, more often than not, your frustrations will be of the more mundane variety. As long as you live here on earth, you will face countless opportunities to lose your temper over small, relatively insignificant events: a traffic jam, a spilled cup of coffee, an inconsiderate comment, a broken promise. When you are tempted to lose your temper over the minor inconveniences of life, don't. Turn away from anger, hatred, bitterness, and regret. Turn instead to God.

Anger unresolved will only bring you woe.

Kay Arthur

There is no sin nor wrong that gives a man such a foretaste of hell in this life as anger and impatience.

St. Catherine of Siena

Is there somebody who's always getting your goat? Talk to the Shepherd.

Anonymous

Life is too short to spend it being
angry, bored, or dull.

Barbara Johnson

If your temper gets the best of you . . . then other people get to see the worst in you.

Marie T. Freeman

Wisdom always waits for the right time to act, while emotion always pushes for action right now.

Joyce Meyer

183

MORE FROM GOD'S WORD

Don't let your spirit rush to be angry, for anger abides in the heart of fools.

Ecclesiastes 7:9 HCSB

My dearly loved brothers, understand this: everyone must be quick to hear, slow to speak, and slow to anger, for man's anger does not accomplish God's righteousness.

James 1:19-20 HCSB

A fool's displeasure is known at once, but whoever ignores an insult is sensible.

Proverbs 12:16 HCSB

But now you must also put away all the following: anger, wrath, malice, slander, and filthy language from your mouth.

Colossians 3:8 HCSB

A gentle answer turns away anger, but a harsh word stirs up wrath.

Proverbs 15:1 HCSB

Who is wise and understanding among you?
Let him show by good conduct that his works
are done in the meekness of wisdom.

James 3:13 NKJV

SHADES OF GRACE

You will never be called upon to give anyone more grace than God has already given you.

Max Lucado

A PRAYER FOR TODAY

Lord, sometimes, I am quick to anger and slow to forgive. But I know, Lord, that You seek abundance and peace for my life. Forgiveness is Your commandment; empower me to follow the example of Your Son Jesus who forgave His persecutors. Today, as I turn away from anger, I will claim the peace that You intend for my life, and I will praise You for Your blessings. Amen

He Is Your Rock

The Lord is my rock and my fortress and my deliverer; the God of my strength, in whom I will trust.

2 Samuel 22:2-3 NKJV

God has promised to protect us, and He intends to keep His promise. In a world filled with dangers and temptations, God is the ultimate armor. In a world filled with misleading messages, God's Word is the ultimate truth. In a world filled with more frustrations than we can count, God's Son offers the ultimate peace.

As a busy woman, you know from firsthand experience that life is not always easy. But as a recipient of God's grace, you also know that you are protected by a loving Heavenly Father.

In times of trouble, God will comfort you; in times of sorrow, He will dry your tears. When you are troubled, or weak, or sorrowful, God is neither distant nor disinterested. To the contrary, God is always present and always vitally engaged in the events of your life. Reach out to Him, and build your future on the rock that cannot be shaken…trust in God and rely upon His provisions. He can provide everything you really need . . . and far, far more.

God provides the ingredients for our daily bread but expects us to do the baking. With our own hands!

Barbara Johnson

He goes before us, follows behind us, and hems us safe inside the realm of His protection.

Beth Moore

We can take great comfort that God never sleeps—so we can.

Dianna Booher

God will never let you sink under your circumstances. He always provide a safety net and His love always encircles.

Barbara Johnson

When you live a surrendered life, God is willing and able to provide for your every need.

Corrie ten Boom

Our God is the sovereign Creator of the universe! He loves us as His own children and has provided every good thing we have; He is worthy of our praise every moment.

Shirley Dobson

Love has its source in God,
for love is the very essence of His being.

Kay Arthur

When terrible things happen, there are two choices, and only two: We can trust God, or we can defy Him. We believe that God is God, He's still got the whole world in His hands and knows exactly what He's doing, or we must believe that He is not God and that we are at the awful mercy of mere chance.

Elisabeth Elliot

I believe that God is in the miracle business—that His favorite way of working is to pick up where our human abilities and understandings leave off and then do something so wondrous and unexpected that there's no doubt who the God is around here.

Emilie Barnes

More from God's Word

I know whom I have believed and am persuaded that He is able to guard what has been entrusted to me until that day.

2 Timothy 1:12 HCSB

For the LORD your God has arrived to live among you. He is a mighty savior. He will rejoice over you with great gladness. With his love, he will calm all your fears. He will exult over you by singing a happy song.

Zephaniah 3:17 HCSB

God—His way is perfect; the word of the Lord is pure. He is a shield to all who take refuge in Him.

Psalm 18:30 HCSB

The Lord bless you and protect you; the Lord make His face shine on you, and be gracious to you.

Numbers 6:24-25 HCSB

And God is able to make all grace abound toward you, that you, always having all sufficiency in all things, may have an abundance for every good work.

2 Corinthians 9:8 NKJV

189

But by means of their suffering,
he rescues those who suffer.
For he gets their attention through adversity.

Job 36:15 NLT

SHADES OF GRACE

The grace of God is infinite and eternal. As it had no beginning, so it can have no end, and being an attribute of God, it is as boundless as infinitude.

A. W. Tozer

A PRAYER FOR TODAY

Lord, You are my Shepherd. You care for me; You comfort me; You watch over me; and You have saved me. I will praise You, Father, for Your glorious works, for Your protection, for Your love, and for Your Son. Amen

Focusing on God, Not Fear

But He said to them, "Why are you fearful, O you of little faith?" Then He arose and rebuked the winds and the sea, and there was a great calm.

Matthew 8:26 NKJV

A frightening storm rose quickly on the Sea of Galilee, and the disciples were afraid. Because of their limited faith, they feared for their lives. When they turned to Jesus, He calmed the waters and He rebuked His disciples for their lack of faith in Him.

On occasion, we, like the disciples, are frightened by the inevitable storms of life. Why are we afraid? Because we, like the disciples, are imperfect and possess imperfect faith.

When we genuinely accept God's promises as absolute truth, when we trust Him with life-here-on-earth and life eternal, we have little to fear. Faith in God is the antidote to worry. Faith in God is the foundation of courage and the source of power. Today, let us trust God more completely and, by doing so, move beyond our fears to a place of abundance, assurance, and peace.

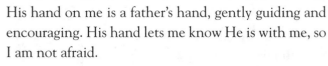

God did away with all my fear. It was time for someone to stand up—or in my case, sit down. So I refused to move.

Rosa Parks

God knows that the strength that comes from wrestling with our fear will give us wings to fly.

Paula Rinehart

His hand on me is a father's hand, gently guiding and encouraging. His hand lets me know He is with me, so I am not afraid.

Mary Morrison Suggs

Fear knocked at the door. Faith answered. No one was there.

Anonymous

Let nothing disturb you, nothing frighten you; all things are passing; God never changes.

St. Teresa of Avila

MORE FROM GOD'S WORD

Even when I go through the darkest valley, I fear [no] danger, for You are with me.

Psalm 23:4 HCSB

Don't be afraid. Only believe.

Mark 5:36 HCSB

For I, the Lord your God, hold your right hand and say to you: Do not fear, I will help you.

Isaiah 41:13 HCSB

I sought the Lord, and He heard me, and delivered me from all my fears.

Psalm 34:4 NKJV

Do not fear, for I am with you; do not be afraid, for I am your God. I will strengthen you; I will help you; I will hold on to you with My righteous right hand.

Isaiah 41:10 HCSB

193

Faith is nothing more or less than
actively trusting God.

Catherine Marshall

SHADES OF GRACE

God shields us from most of the things we fear,
but when He chooses not to shield us, He un-
failingly allots grace in the measure needed.

Elisabeth Elliot

A PRAYER FOR TODAY

*Father, even when I walk through the valley of the shadow
of death, I will fear no evil because You are with me. Thank
You, Lord, for Your perfect love, a love that casts out fear
and gives me strength and courage to meet the challenges
of this world. Amen*

Your Reasons to Rejoice

Set your minds on what is above, not on what is on the earth.

Colossians 3:2 HCSB

The Christian life is a cause for celebration, but sometimes we don't feel much like celebrating. In fact, when the weight of the world seems to bear down upon our shoulders, celebration may be the last thing on our minds . . . but it shouldn't be. As God's children, we are all blessed beyond measure on good days and bad. This day is a non-renewable resource—once it's gone, it's gone forever. We should give thanks for this day while using it for the glory of God.

What will be your attitude today? Will you be fearful, angry, bored, or worried? Will you be cynical, bitter, or pessimistic? If so, God wants to have a little talk with you.

God created you in His own image, and He wants you to experience joy and abundance. But, God will not force His joy upon you; you must claim it for yourself. So today, and every day hereafter, celebrate the life that God has given you. Think optimistically about yourself and your future. Give thanks to the One who has given you everything, and trust in your heart that He wants to give you so much more.

Each one of us is responsible for our own happiness. If we choose to allow ourselves to become miserable and unhappy, the problem is ours, not someone else's.

Joyce Meyer

I could go through this day oblivious to the miracles all around me, or I could tune in and "enjoy."

Gloria Gaither

The things we think are the things that feed our souls. If we think on pure and lovely things, we shall grow pure and lovely like them; and the converse is equally true.

Hannah Whitall Smith

Optimism is that faith that leads to achievement. Nothing can be done without hope and confidence.

Helen Keller

MORE FROM GOD'S WORD

For the word of God is living and active. Sharper than any double-edged sword, it penetrates even to dividing soul and spirit, joints and marrow; it judges the thoughts and attitudes of the heart.

Hebrews 4:12 NIV

Therefore, since Christ suffered in his body, arm yourselves also with the same attitude, because he who has suffered in his body is done with sin. As a result, he does not live the rest of his earthly life for evil human desires, but rather for the will of God.

1 Peter 4:1-2 NIV

Your attitude should be the same as that of Christ Jesus: Who, being in very nature God, did not consider equality with God something to be grasped, but made himself nothing, taking the very nature of a servant, being made in human likeness. And being found in appearance as a man, he humbled himself and became obedient to death—even death on a cross!

Philippians 2:5-8 NIV

A miserable heart means a miserable life;
a cheerful heart fills the day with a song.

Proverbs 15:15 MSG

SHADES OF GRACE

When I consider my existence beyond the grace, I am filled with confidence and gratitude because God has made an inviolable commitment to take me to heaven on the merits of Christ.

Bill Hybels

A PRAYER FOR TODAY

Lord, I have so many reasons to be thankful; let my attitude be a reflection of the many blessings I have received. Make me a woman whose thoughts are Christlike and whose hopes are worthy of the One who has given me so much. Amen

The Power of Perseverance

If you do nothing in a difficult time, your strength is limited.
Proverbs 24:10 HCSB

In a world filled with roadblocks and stumbling blocks, we need strength, courage, and perseverance. And, as an example of perfect perseverance, we need look no further than our Savior, Jesus Christ.

Jesus finished what He began. Despite the torture He endured, despite the shame of the cross, Jesus was steadfast in His faithfulness to God. We, too, must remain faithful, especially during times of hardship.

Perhaps you are in a hurry for God to reveal His plans for your life. If so, be forewarned: God operates on His own timetable, not yours. Sometimes, God may answer your prayers with silence, and when He does, you must patiently persevere. In times of trouble, you must remain steadfast and trust in the merciful goodness of your Heavenly Father. Whatever your problem, He can handle it. Your job is to keep persevering until He does.

We ought to make some progress, however little, every day, and show some increase of fervor. We ought to act as if we were at war—as, indeed, we are—and never relax until we have won the victory.

St. Teresa of Avila

If all things are possible with God, then all things are possible to him who believes in Him.

Corrie ten Boom

Are you a Christian? If you are, how can you be hopeless? Are you so depressed by the greatness of your problems that you have given up all hope? Instead of giving up, would you patiently endure? Would you focus on Christ until you are so preoccupied with Him alone that you fall prostrate before Him?

Anne Graham Lotz

Failure is one of life's most powerful teachers. How we handle our failures determines whether we're going to simply "get by" in life or "press on."

Beth Moore

Your life is not a boring stretch of highway. It's a straight line to heaven. And just look at the fields ripening along the way. Look at the tenacity and endurance. Look at the grains of righteousness. You'll have quite a crop at harvest...so don't give up!

Joni Eareckson Tada

The most profane word we use is "hopeless." When you say a situation or person is hopeless, you are slamming the door in the face of God.

Kathy Troccoli

We can do anything we want to do if we stick to it long enough.

Helen Keller

The amount of power you experience to live a victorious, triumphant Christian life is directly proportional to the freedom you give the Spirit to be Lord of your life!

Anne Graham Lotz

God provides the ingredients for our daily bread but expects us to do the baking. With our own hands!

Barbara Johnson

201

MORE FROM GOD'S WORD

I leave you peace; my peace I give you. I do not give it to you as the world does. So don't let your hearts be troubled or afraid.

John 14:27 NCV

If your sinful nature controls your mind, there is death. But if the Holy Spirit controls your mind, there is life and peace.

Romans 8:6 NLT

If it is possible, as far as it depends on you, live at peace with everyone.

Romans 12:18 NIV

Blessed are the peacemakers, for they will be called sons of God.

Matthew 5:9 NIV

Do not lack diligence; be fervent in spirit; serve the Lord.

Romans 12:11 HCSB

*Even though good people may be
bothered by trouble seven times,
they are never defeated.*

Proverbs 24:16 NCV

SHADES OF GRACE

What grace calls you to do, grace provides.
Grace is power.

Kay Arthur

A PRAYER FOR TODAY

*Lord, when life is difficult, I am tempted to abandon
hope in the future. But You are my God, and I can draw
strength from You. Let me trust You, Father, in good times
and in bad times. Let me persevere—even if my soul is
troubled—and let me follow Your Son, Jesus Christ, this
day and forever. Amen*

The Light of the World

I have come as a light into the world, so that everyone who believes in Me would not remain in darkness.

John 12:46 HCSB

The Bible says that you are "the light that gives light to the world." The Bible also says that you should live in a way that lets other people understand what it means to be a follower of Jesus.

What kind of light have you been giving off? Hopefully, you've been a good example for everybody to see. Why? Because the world needs all the light it can get, and that includes your light, too!

The old familiar hymn begins, "What a friend we have in Jesus . . . ." No truer words were ever penned. Jesus is the sovereign Friend and ultimate Savior of mankind. Christ showed enduring love for you by willingly sacrificing His own life so that you might have eternal life. As a response to His sacrifice, you should love Him, praise Him, and share His message of salvation with your family, your friends, your neighbors and with the world.

Do you seek to be an extreme follower of Christ? Then you must let your light shine . . . today and every day.

If we guard some corner of darkness in ourselves, we will soon be drawing someone else into darkness, shutting them out from the light in the face of Jesus Christ.

Elisabeth Elliot

You have to look for the joy. Look for the light of God that is hitting your life, and you will find sparkles you didn't know were there.

Barbara Johnson

If we do not radiate the light of Christ around us, the sense of the darkness that prevails in the world will increase.

Mother Teresa

God's guidance is even more important than common sense. I can declare that the deepest darkness is outshone by the light of Jesus.

Corrie ten Boom

More from God's Word

You are the light that gives light to the world...Live so that they will see the good things you do. Live so that they will praise your Father in heaven.

Matthew 5:14,16 ICB

Then Jesus spoke to them again: "I am the light of the world. Anyone who follows Me will never walk in the darkness, but will have the light of life."

John 8:12 HCSB

Take My yoke upon you and learn from Me, because I am gentle and humble in heart, and you will find rest for your souls. For My yoke is easy and My burden is light.

Matthew 11:29-30 HCSB

How happy is everyone who fears the Lord, who walks in His ways!

Psalm 128:1 HCSB

For me, living is Christ and dying is gain.

Philippians 1:21 HCSB

His life is our light—our purpose and
meaning and reason for living.

Anne Graham Lotz

SHADES OF GRACE

Costly grace is the treasure hidden in the field;
for the sake of it, a man will gladly go and sell
all that he has. It is costly because it costs a man
his life, and it is grace because it gives a man the
only true life.

Dietrich Bonhoeffer

A PRAYER FOR TODAY

*Heavenly Father, I praise You for Your Son Jesus, the light
of the world and my personal Savior. Let me share His
Good News with all who cross my path, and let me share
His love with all who need His healing touch. Amen*

His Truth

You will know the truth, and the truth will set you free.

John 8:32 HCSB

God is vitally concerned with truth. His Word teaches the truth; His Spirit reveals the truth; His Son leads us to the truth. When we open our hearts to God, and when we allow His Son to rule over our thoughts and our lives, God reveals Himself, and we come to understand the truth about ourselves and the Truth (with a capital T) about God's gift of grace.

The familiar words of John 8:32 remind us that when we come to know God's Truth, we are liberated. Have you been liberated by that Truth? And are you living in accordance with the eternal truths that you find in God's Holy Word? Hopefully so.

Today, as you fulfill the responsibilities that God has placed before you, ask yourself this question: "Do my thoughts and actions bear witness to the ultimate Truth that God has placed in my heart, or am I allowing the pressures of everyday life to overwhelm me?" It's a profound question that deserves an answer . . . now.

The difficult truth about truth is that it often requires us to change our perspectives, attitudes, and rules for living.

Susan Lenzkes

To worship Him in truth means to worship Him honestly, without hypocrisy, standing open and transparent before Him.

Anne Graham Lotz

Those who walk in truth walk in liberty.

Beth Moore

The Holy Spirit was given to guide us into all truth, but He doesn't do it all at once.

Elisabeth Elliot

209

MORE FROM GOD'S WORD

"You are a king then?" Pilate asked. "You say that I'm a king," Jesus replied. "I was born for this, and I have come into the world for this: to testify to the truth. Everyone who is of the truth listens to My voice."

John 18:37 HCSB

For God's wrath is revealed from heaven against all godlessness and unrighteousness of people who by their unrighteousness suppress the truth.

Romans 1:18 HCSB

These are the things you must do: Speak truth to one another; render honest and peaceful judgments in your gates.

Zechariah 8:16 HCSB

Be diligent to present yourself approved to God, a worker who doesn't need to be ashamed, correctly teaching the word of truth.

2 Timothy 2:15 HCSB

When the Spirit of truth comes, He will guide you into all the truth.

John 16:13 HCSB

Either God's Word keeps you from sin,
or sin keeps you from God's Word.

Corrie ten Boom

SHADES OF GRACE

Though the details may differ from story to story, we are all sinners—saved only by the wonderful grace of God.

Gloria Gaither

A PRAYER FOR TODAY

Heavenly Father, You are the way and the truth and the light. Today—as I follow Your way and share Your Good News—let me be a worthy example to others and a worthy servant to You. Amen

The Power of Patience

The Lord is wonderfully good to those who wait for him and seek him. So it is good to wait quietly for salvation from the Lord.

Lamentations 3:25-26 NLT

Are you a woman in a hurry? If so, you may be in for a few disappointments. Why? Because life has a way of unfolding according to its own timetable, not yours. That's why life requires patience . . . and lots of it!

Most of us are impatient for God to grant us the desires of our heart. Usually, we know what we want, and we know precisely when we want it: right now, if not sooner. But God may have other plans. And when God's plans differ from our own, we must trust in His infinite wisdom and in His infinite love.

Lamentations 3:25 reminds us that, "The Lord is wonderfully good to those who wait for him and seek him" (NIV). But, for most of us, waiting quietly is difficult because we're in such a hurry for things to happen!

The next time you find your patience tested to the limit, slow down, take a deep breath, and relax. Sometimes life can't be hurried—and during those times, patience is indeed a priceless virtue.

How do you wait upon the Lord? First you must learn to sit at His feet and take time to listen to His words.

Kay Arthur

When we read of the great Biblical leaders, we see that it was not uncommon for God to ask them to wait, not just a day or two, but for years, until God was ready for them to act.

Gloria Gaither

We must learn to wait. There is grace supplied to the one who waits.

Mrs. Charles E. Cowman

Let me encourage you to continue to wait with faith. God may not perform a miracle, but He is trustworthy to touch you and make you whole where there used to be a hole.

Lisa Whelchel

213

Waiting is the hardest kind of work, but God knows best, and we may joyfully leave all in His hands.

Lottie Moon

Wisdom always waits for the right time to act, while emotion always pushes for action right now.

Joyce Meyer

God's peace is like a river, not a pond. In other words, a sense of health and well-being, both of which are expressions of the Hebrew *shalom*, can permeate our homes even when we're in white-water rapids.

Beth Moore

We are so used to living in an instant world that it is difficult to wait for anything.

Kay Arthur

God's delays and His ways can be confusing because the process God uses to accomplish His will can go against human logic and common sense.

Anne Graham Lotz

MORE FROM GOD'S WORD

Rejoice in hope; be patient in affliction; be persistent in prayer.

Romans 12:12 HCSB

Love is patient; love is kind.

1 Corinthians 13:4 HCSB

A patient spirit is better than a proud spirit.

Ecclesiastes 7:8 HCSB

Therefore the Lord is waiting to show you mercy, and is rising up to show you compassion, for the Lord is a just God. Happy are all who wait patiently for Him.

Isaiah 30:18 HCSB

A patient person [shows] great understanding, but a quick-tempered one promotes foolishness.

Proverbs 14:29 HCSB

I wait for the Lord; I wait, and put my hope in His word.

Psalm 130:5 HCSB

215

To everything there is a season,
a time for every purpose under heaven.

Ecclesiastes 3:1 NKJV

SHADES OF GRACE

God does amazing works through prayers that seek to extend His grace to others.

Shirley Dobson

A PRAYER FOR TODAY

Lord, give me patience. When I am hurried, give me peace. When I am frustrated, give me perspective. When I am angry, let me turn my heart to You. Today, let me become a more patient woman, Dear Lord, as I trust in You and in Your master plan for my life. Amen

Following Christ

But whoever keeps His word, truly in him the love of God is perfected. This is how we know we are in Him: the one who says he remains in Him should walk just as He walked.

1 John 2:5-6 HCSB

J esus walks with you. Are you walking with Him? Hopefully, you will choose to walk with Him today and every day of your life.

Jesus loved you so much that He endured unspeakable humiliation and suffering for you. How will you respond to Christ's sacrifice? Will you take up His cross and follow Him (Luke 9:23), or will you choose another path? When you place your hopes squarely at the foot of the cross, when you place Jesus squarely at the center of your life, you will be blessed. If you seek to be a worthy disciple of Jesus, you must acknowledge that He never comes "next." He is always first.

Do you hope to fulfill God's purpose for your life? Do you seek a life of abundance and peace? Do you intend to be Christian, not just in name, but in deed?

Then follow Christ. Follow Him by picking up His cross today and every day that you live. When you do, you will quickly discover that Christ's love has the power to change everything, including you.

As we live moment by moment under the control of the Spirit, His character, which is the character of Jesus, becomes evident to those around us.

Anne Graham Lotz

Will you, with a glad and eager surrender, hand yourself and all that concerns you over into His hands? If you will do this, your soul will begin to know something of the joy of union with Christ.

Hannah Whitall Smith

Peter said, "No, Lord!" But he had to learn that one cannot say "No" while saying "Lord" and that one cannot say "Lord" while saying "No."

Corrie ten Boom

Think of this—we may live together with Him here and now, a daily walking with Him who loved us and gave Himself for us.

Elisabeth Elliot

Blessed assurance, Jesus is mine! O what a foretaste of glory divine!

Fanny Crosby

Knowing where you are going takes the uncertainty out of getting there.

Anne Graham Lotz

219

MORE FROM GOD'S WORD

*Then he told them what they could expect for themselves:
"Anyone who intends to come with me has to let me lead."*

Luke 9:23 MSG

I've laid down a pattern for you. What I've done, you do.

John 13:15 MSG

*No one can serve two masters. Either he will hate the one
and love the other, or he will be devoted to the one and
despise the other.*

Matthew 6:24 NIV

*Whoever is not willing to carry the cross and follow me is
not worthy of me. Those who try to hold on to their lives
will give up true life. Those who give up their lives for me
will hold on to true life.*

Matthew 10:38-39 NCV

*If anyone would come after me, he must deny himself and
take up his cross and follow me.*

Mark 8:34 NIV

*For the Son of Man has come to save
that which was lost.*

Matthew 18:11 NKJV

SHADES OF GRACE

The supreme force in salvation is God's grace.
Not our works. Not our talents. Not our feelings. Not our strength.

Max Lucado

A PRAYER FOR TODAY

*Dear Lord, You sent Your Son so that I might have
abundant life and eternal life. I praise You, Father, for my
Savior, Christ Jesus. I will follow Him, honor Him, and
share His Good News, this day and every day. Amen*

Praising Him for This Day

Teach us to number our days carefully so that we may develop wisdom in our hearts.

Psalm 90:12 HCSB

This day is a gift from God. How will you use it? Will you celebrate God's gifts and obey His commandments? Will you share words of encouragement and hope with all who cross your path? Will you trust in the Father and praise His glorious handiwork? The answer to these questions will determine, to a surprising extent, the direction and the quality of your day.

The familiar words of Psalm 118:24 remind us of a profound yet simple truth: "This is the day which the LORD hath made; we will rejoice and be glad in it" (KJV). For Christian believers, every day begins and ends with God and His Son. Christ came to this earth to give us abundant life and eternal salvation. We give thanks to our Maker when we treasure each day and use it to the fullest.

Today, may we give thanks for this day and for the One who created it.

Each day, each moment is so pregnant with eternity that if we "tune in" to it, we can hardly contain the joy.

Gloria Gaither

Every day of our lives we make choices about how we're going to live that day.

Luci Swindoll

Every day we live is a priceless gift of God, loaded with possibilities to learn something new, to gain fresh insights.

Dale Evans Rogers

Today is mine. Tomorrow is none of my business. If I peer anxiously into the fog of the future, I will strain my spiritual eyes so that I will not see clearly what is required of me now.

Elisabeth Elliot

Give yourself a gift today: be present with yourself. God is. Enjoy your own personality. God does.

Barbara Johnson

MORE FROM GOD'S WORD

This is the day the Lord has made; let us rejoice and be glad in it.

Psalm 118:24 HCSB

Rejoice in the Lord always. I will say it again: Rejoice!

Philippians 4:4 HCSB

I must work the works of Him who sent Me while it is day; the night is coming when no one can work.

John 9:4 NKJV

Therefore, get your minds ready for action, being self-disciplined, and set your hope completely on the grace to be brought to you at the revelation of Jesus Christ.

1 Peter 1:13 HCSB

Working together with Him, we also appeal to you: "Don't receive God's grace in vain." For He says: In an acceptable time, I heard you, and in the day of salvation, I helped you. Look, now is the acceptable time; look, now is the day of salvation.

2 Corinthians 6:1-2 HCSB

Submit each day to God, knowing that
He is God over all your tomorrows.

Kay Arthur

SHADES OF GRACE

The life of faith is a daily exploration of the
constant and countless ways in which God's
grace and love are experienced.

Eugene Peterson

A PRAYER FOR TODAY

*Lord, You have given me another day of life; let me
celebrate this day, and let me use it according to Your plan.
I praise You, Father, for my life and for the friends and
family members who make it rich. Enable me to live each
moment to the fullest as I give thanks for Your creation, for
Your love, and for Your Son. Amen*

Trust Him

Trust in the LORD with all your heart; do not depend on your own understanding. Seek his will in all you do, and he will direct your paths.

Proverbs 3:5-6 NLT

O pen your Bible to its center, and you'll find the Book of Psalms. In it are some of the most beautiful words ever translated into the English language, with none more beautiful than the 23rd Psalm. David describes God as being like a shepherd who cares for His flock. No wonder these verses have provided comfort and hope for generations of believers.

On occasion, you will confront circumstances that trouble you to the very core of your soul. When you are afraid, trust in God. When you are worried, turn your concerns over to Him. When you are anxious, be still and listen for the quiet assurance of God's promises. And then, place your life in His hands. He is your shepherd today and throughout eternity. Trust the Shepherd.

The only safe place is in the center of God's will. It is not only the safest place. It is also the most rewarding and the most satisfying place to be.

Gigi Graham Tchividjian

Obedience is a foundational stepping stone on the path of God's Will.

Elizabeth George

I believe that in every time and place it is within our power to acquiesce in the will of God—and what peace it brings to do so!

Elisabeth Elliot

In the Garden of Gethsemane, Jesus went through agony of soul in His efforts to resist the temptation to do what He felt like doing rather than what He knew was God's will for Him.

Joyce Meyer

The will of God is the most delicious and delightful thing in the universe.

Hannah Whitall Smith

227

The center of power is not to be found in summit meetings or in peace conferences. It is not in Peking or Washington or the United Nations, but rather where a child of God prays in the power of the Spirit for God's will to be done in her life, in her home, and in the world around her.

Ruth Bell Graham

When we reach the end of our strength, wisdom, and personal resources, we enter into the beginning of his glorious provisions.

Patsy Clairmont

The strength that we claim from God's Word does not depend on circumstances. Circumstances will be difficult, but our strength will be sufficient.

Corrie ten Boom

Do not limit the limitless God! With Him, face the future unafraid because you are never alone.

Mrs. Charles E. Cowman

MORE FROM GOD'S WORD

Let us hold fast the confession of our hope without wavering, for He who promised is faithful.

Hebrews 10:23 NKJV

For we walk by faith, not by sight.

2 Corinthians 5:7 NKJV

The one who understands a matter finds success, and the one who trusts in the Lord will be happy.

Proverbs 16:20 HCSB

For the eyes of the Lord range throughout the earth to show Himself strong for those whose hearts are completely His.

2 Chronicles 16:9 HCSB

Give your burdens to the Lord, and he will take care of you. He will not permit the godly to slip and fall.

Psalm 55:22 NLT

I wait quietly before God, for my salvation comes from him. He alone is my rock and my salvation, my fortress where I will never be shaken.

Psalm 62:1-2 NLT

229

*He granted their request because
they trusted in Him.*

1 Chronicles 5:20 HCSB

SHADES OF GRACE

Jesus has affected human society like no other.
The incomparable Christ is the good news. And
what makes it such good news is that man is so
undeserving but that God is so gracious.

John MacArthur

A PRAYER FOR TODAY

*Lord, when I trust in things of this earth, I will be
disappointed. But, when I put my faith in You, I am
secure. You are my rock and my shield. Upon Your firm
foundation I will build my life. When I am worried, Lord,
let me trust in You. You will love me and protect me, and
You will share Your boundless grace today, tomorrow, and
forever. Amen*

The Priceless Gift of Eternal Life

For God so loved the world that He gave His only begotten Son, that whoever believes in Him should not perish but have everlasting life.

John 3:16 NKJV

Ours is not a distant God. Ours is a God who understands—far better than we ever could—the essence of what it means to be human. How marvelous it is that God became a man and walked among us. Had He not chosen to do so, we might feel removed from a distant Creator.

God understands our hopes, our fears, and our temptations. He understands what it means to be angry and what it costs to forgive. He knows the heart, the conscience, and the soul of every person who has ever lived, including you. And God has a plan of salvation that is intended for you. Accept it. Accept God's gift through the person of His Son Christ Jesus, and then rest assured: God walked among us so that you might have eternal life; amazing though it may seem, He did it for you.

If you are a believer, your judgment will not determine your eternal destiny. Christ's finished work on Calvary was applied to you the moment you accepted Christ as Savior.

Beth Moore

> Your choice to either receive or reject the Lord Jesus Christ will determine where you spend eternity.
>
> *Anne Graham Lotz*

It is in giving that we receive, it is in pardoning that we are pardoned, it is in dying that we are born to eternal life.

St. Francis

The end will be glorious beyond our wildest dreams—for those who put their trust in Him.

Elisabeth Elliot

The gift of God is eternal life, spiritual life, abundant life through faith in Jesus Christ, the Living Word of God.

Anne Graham Lotz

God has promised us abundance, peace, and eternal life. These treasures are ours for the asking; all we must do is claim them. One of the great mysteries of life is why on earth do so many of us wait so very long to lay claim to God's gifts?

Marie T. Freeman

Finally, ultimately, eternally, our dream of living in a home that is paid for will be realized, because Jesus has paid it all!

Anne Graham Lotz

I can still hardly believe it. I, with shriveled, bent fingers, atrophied muscles, gnarled knees, and no feeling from the shoulders down, will one day have a new body—light, bright and clothed in righteousness—powerful and dazzling.

Joni Eareckson Tada

MORE FROM GOD'S WORD

And this is the testimony: God has given us eternal life, and this life is in His Son. The one who has the Son has life. The one who doesn't have the Son of God does not have life.

1 John 5:11-12 HCSB

Jesus said to her, "I am the resurrection and the life. The one who believes in Me, even if he dies, will live. Everyone who lives and believes in Me will never die—ever. Do you believe this?"

John 11:25-26 HCSB

I have written these things to you who believe in the name of the Son of God, so that you may know that you have eternal life.

1 John 5:13 HCSB

And this is the will of Him who sent Me, that everyone who sees the Son and believes in Him may have everlasting life; and I will raise him up at the last day.

John 6:40 NKJV

Our citizenship is in heaven, from which we also eagerly wait for a Savior, the Lord Jesus Christ.

Philippians 3:20 HCSB

As you go, announce this:
"The kingdom of heaven has come near."

Matthew 10:7 HCSB

SHADES OF GRACE

Just as I am, without one plea, but that Thy blood was shed for me. And that Thou bid'st me come to Thee, O Lamb of God, I come! I come!

Charlotte Elliott

A PRAYER FOR TODAY

Lord, I am only here on this earth for a brief while. But, You have offered me the priceless gift of eternal life through Your Son Jesus. I accept Your gift, Lord, with thanksgiving and praise. Let me share the good news of my salvation with those who need Your healing touch. Amen

Putting God First

Honor GOD with everything you own; give him the first and the best. Your barns will burst, your wine vats will brim over.

Proverbs 3:9-10 MSG

As you think about the nature of your relationship with God, remember this: you will always have some type of relationship with Him—it is inevitable that your life must be lived in relationship to God. The question is not if you will have a relationship with Him; the burning question is whether or not that relationship will be one that seeks to honor Him . . . or not.

Are you willing to place God first in your life? And, are you willing to welcome God's Son into your heart? Unless you can honestly answer these questions with a resounding yes, then your relationship with God isn't what it could be or should be. Thankfully, God is always available, He's always ready to forgive, and He's waiting to hear from you now. The rest, of course, is up to you.

Make God's will the focus of your life day by day. If you seek to please Him and Him alone, you'll find yourself satisfied with life.

Kay Arthur

Jesus challenges you and me to keep our focus daily on the cross of His will if we want to be His disciples.

Anne Graham Lotz

The greatest honor you can give Almighty God is to live gladly and joyfully because of the knowledge of His love.

Juliana of Norwich

The Holy Spirit testifies of Jesus. So when you are filled with the Holy Spirit, you speak about our Lord and really live to His honor.

Corrie ten Boom

Whatever may be our circumstances in life, may each one of us really believe that by way of the Throne we have unlimited power.

Annie Armstrong

Since we're only human, understanding God is out of the question. But trusting Him is not.

Marie T. Freeman

Spiritual worship is focusing all we are on all He is.

Beth Moore

The manifold rewards of a serious, consistent prayer life demonstrate clearly that time with our Lord should be our first priority.

Shirley Dobson

I lived with Indians who made pots out of clay which they used for cooking. Nobody was interested in the pot. Everybody was interested in what was inside. The same clay taken out of the same riverbed, always made in the same design, nothing special about it. Well, I'm a clay pot, and let me not forget it. But, the excellency of the power is of God and not us.

Elisabeth Elliot

MORE FROM GOD'S WORD

You shall have no other gods before Me.

Exodus 20:3 NKJV

Jesus answered, "'Love the Lord your God with all your heart, all your soul, and all your mind.' This is the first and most important command."

Matthew 22:37-38 NCV

Those who worship false gods turn their backs on all God's mercies. But I will offer sacrifices to you with songs of praise, and I will fulfill all my vows. For my salvation comes from the LORD alone.

Jonah 2:8-9 NLT

The Devil said to Him, "I will give You their splendor and all this authority, because it has been given over to me, and I can give it to anyone I want. If You, then, will worship me, all will be Yours." And Jesus answered him, "It is written: You shall worship the Lord your God, and Him alone you shall serve."

Luke 4:6-8 HCSB

To you, O Lord, I lift up my soul. I trust in you, my God.

Psalm 25:1-2 NLT

*Happy are those who hear the joyful call
to worship, for they will walk in the light
of your presence, Lord.*

Psalm 89:15 NLT

SHADES OF GRACE

Thank God, He does not measure grace out in
teaspoons.

Amy Carmichael

A PRAYER FOR TODAY

*Dear Lord, Your love is eternal and Your laws are
everlasting. When I obey Your commandments, I am
blessed. Today, I invite You to reign over every corner of
my heart. I will have faith in You, Father. I will sense Your
presence; I will accept Your love; I will trust Your will; and
I will praise You for the Savior of my life: Your Son Jesus.
Amen*